Juan Rulfo

Twayne's World Authors Series

Luis Dávila, Editor
Indiana University, Bloomington

TWAS 692

JUAN RULFO
Photograph by Rafael López Castro
Reproduced by permission of the Fondo de Cultura Económica.

Juan Rulfo

By Luis Leal

*University of California,
Santa Barbara*

Twayne Publishers • *Boston*

Juan Rulfo

Luis Leal

Book Production by Marne B. Sultz

Book Design by Barbara Anderson

Short passages from Juan Rulfo's *Pedro Páramo* are
reprinted by permission of Grove Press, Inc.
Translated from the Spanish by Lysander Kemp.
Copyright © 1959 by Grove Press, Inc., and from
The Burning Plain by permission of the University
of Texas Press. Translated by George D. Schade.
Copyright © 1967 by the University of Texas
Press.

Printed on permanent/durable acid-free
paper and bound in the United States of
America.

**Library of Congress Cataloging in
Publication Data**

Leal, Luis, 1907–
Juan Rulfo.

(Twayne's world authors series ; TWAS
692)
Bibliography: p. 116
Includes index.
1. Rulfo, Juan—Criticism and
interpretation.
I. Title. II. Series.
PQ7297.R89Z75 1983 863 83-40
ISBN 0-8057-6539-5

A
la memoria
de mi padre
Luis Leal Ardines

Contents

About the Author

Luis Leal, born in Mexico, received the B.S. from Northwestern University, and the M.A. and Ph.D. from the University of Chicago. In 1976 he retired from the University of Illinois and has since been Visiting Professor of Spanish at the University of California, Santa Barbara. At the present time he is also Acting Director of the Center for Chicano Studies at UCSB. He has published numerous books, among them *México, civilizaciones y culturas* (1955; 2d ed., 1971); *Breve historia del cuento mexicano* (1957); *Bibliografía del cuento mexicano* (1958); *La Revolución y las Letras* (with Edmundo Valadés, 1961); *Historia del cuento hispanoamericano* (1966; 2d ed., 1971); *Panorama de la literatura mexicana actual* (1968); *Breve historia de la literatura hispanoamericana* (1971); and *Cuentos de la Revolución* (1977). He has contributed to the *Encyclopaedia Britannica*, the *Gran Enciclopedia Rialp*, and the *Handbook of Latin American Studies*. He has published over 200 articles in leading journals, both in the United States and Latin America, and has lectured extensively at leading universities. In 1978 Donald W. Bleznick and Juan O. Valencia edited an *Homenaje a Luis Leal: estudios sobre literatura hispanoamericana*, published in Madrid by Insula.

Preface

Juan Rulfo has published only three slender volumes of fiction, yet his name has become well known throughout the literary world. The fact that his works capture the very essence of Mexico—its geography, its people—may explain his popularity. But there is the added factor that his novel *Pedro Páramo,* published in 1955, introduced a new type of fiction that was soon to explode with a "boom" in Latin America.

Unlike the fiction of other new writers, Rulfo's novel was not well received at first. Critics either did not understand it or did not want to invest time trying to penetrate the complex structure of a seemingly simple plot, the life of a common *cacique* living in a small town in a desolated region of Mexico. This was not the case with his short stories published two years earlier, which were acclaimed by critics as representing a new trend in the development of the Mexican short narrative, a trend unlike that followed by Juan José Arreola and the imitators of Jorge Luis Borges. Rulfo did not abandon the well-known nativist trend in Spanish American fiction, but, instead, brought it up to date by utilizing new techniques and new ways of presenting Mexican reality.

Not much time elapsed before critics realized that *Pedro Páramo* was indeed a unique novel and worthy of study, not only for its innovative, complex structure, but also for its poetic language and tragic view of life. With the years, the novel has attracted the attention of scholars throughout the world and is now considered a modern classic.

Unlike Mariano Azuela, a fellow native of Jalisco whose novels strongly criticize the government, social institutions, corruption, and the basic weaknesses in the character of the Mexican people, Rulfo usually writes without any ulterior motive. His main preoccupation is to create a literature of aesthetic value, and the social criticism found in his works is a by-product. For this reason he is constantly rewriting and polishing his work until he is satisfied that it is as near perfection as it possibly could be. It is this strict discipline that has probably prevented him from publishing extensively. What he has done, however, has been sufficient to gain for him a world-wide reputation as a great fiction writer.

My purpose here is to present as complete a study of Rulfo's life and works as possible. An attempt has been made to integrate these two aspects of the study by making reference, when discussing his fiction, to historical and sociological phenomena. The study of Rulfo's short fiction has been divided into three chapters, one dedicated to his early writings and the other two to his collection of short stories, *The Burning Plain*, where the stories have been divided into two groups according to date of publication. The study of the novel has been divided into two chapters, one dedicated to its context and genesis, and the other to its imagery and structure. An added chapter deals with Rulfo's latest work, the short novel *El gallo de oro*, and some film scripts that he prepared.

For the quotations from Rulfo's works and those of his critics, available translations have been used whenever possible. If unavailable, the translations are my own. Since Rulfo's critical bibliography has become unusually extensive, it has been impractical to include all existing items. The interested reader can consult the four bibliographies of Rulfo which are listed as secondary sources at the end of the book.

Luis Leal

University of California,
Santa Barbara

Acknowledgments

I would like to acknowledge my gratitude to my wife, Gladys, for her invaluable help in the reading of the manuscript. I would also like to express my thanks to Roberto Trujillo, Director of the Colección Tloque Nahuaque of the Library at the University of California, Santa Barbara, for his help in my search for materials; to Luis Dávila of Indiana University for his encouraging words; and to Wanda Michalenko for her typing of the manuscript.

I thank the University of Texas Press and Grove Press for giving me permission to quote from the translations of *The Burning Plain* and *Pedro Páramo*.

Chronology

a collection of short stories. Resigns from F. G. Goodrich.

1955 Publishes *Pedro Páramo*, first novel; accepts position with the Comisión de Papaloapan in Veracruz State. Film *Talpa* based on story of same name.

1956 Returns to Mexico City.

1958 In charge of Library Archives at the Sociedad Mexicana de Geografía y Estadística. German translation of *Pedro Páramo*; French translation of *El llano en llamas*.

1959 Returns to Guadalajara with wife and children; works at Televicentro; edits historical work; English and French translations of *Pedro Páramo*.

1960 Writes script for film *El despojo*.

1962 Writes narrative sequence for film *Paloma herida*; returns to Mexico City; begins work at Instituto Nacional Indigenista, a position still held.

1963 Italian translation of *El llano en llamas*.

1964 Member Editorial Board *El Cuento. Revista de Imaginación*; unpublished novel *El gallo de oro* made into a film; writes part of text for film *La fórmula secreta*; German translation of *El llano en llamas*.

1966 Motion picture *Pedro Páramo*, with John Gavin.

1967 English translation of *El llano en llamas*.

1970 Receives Premio Nacional de Letras; second edition of *El llano en llamas*, with two new stories.

1971 Travels throughout Europe and Latin America.

1972 *El rincón de las vírgenes*, film based on two of his stories.

1974 Film based on story "No oyes ladrar los perros."

1976 Second filming of *Pedro Páramo*.

1978 Publishes *Antología personal*.

1980 Publishes *El gallo de oro*. Admitted to the Academia Mexicana de la Lengua. Homenaje nacional by Instituto Nacional de Bellas Artes. Publication of special editions of *Pedro Páramo* and *El llano en llamas*.

1982 Juan Rulfo at Barnard.

Chapter One

Son of Affliction: Rulfo's Life and Times

Introduction

Although Mexico had existed as an independent nation since 1821, the first real change in the structure of its society was not brought about until 1857 with the new Constitution based on Benito Juárez's Laws of Reform. That Constitution provided, for the first time, for free elections, the separation of church and state, religious liberty, freedom of speech, the abolition of all titles of nobility, and equality among all citizens regardless of whether they were Indians, *mestizos,* or *criollos* (Spanish descendants).

The changes introduced by Juárez were not accepted without a struggle. The conservatives, unhappy with the liberal Constitution, took up arms in December of 1857, thus launching the War of Reform, or Three Years' War. The country was physically exhausted and economically bankrupt, so President Juárez in 1861 stopped payments on all foreign debts. France, England, and Spain decided to intervene. England and Spain, however, soon withdrew from the alliance, leaving only France to land at Veracruz. After a temporary setback at Puebla on 5 May 1862, the French Army took Mexico City. The conservatives, now in power, decided to abandon the republican form of government for a monarchy and, with the help of Napoleon III, set up the second Mexican Empire during the nineteenth century, with Maximilian of Austria on the throne. But Juárez did not give up so easily and finally conquered Maximilian in 1867, thus reestablishing the Republic. Soon, however, the country fell under the spell of Porfirio Díaz, who ruled as dictator for thirty years. Although Díaz was a follower of the liberals, the basic changes envisioned by Juárez were not put into effect. It is true, however, that Díaz introduced some changes, such as modernizing the country and building railroads. His government was in the hands of a group of intellectuals called *los científicos,* who

1

adopted Positivism and introduced in the schools an education based on scientific knowledge, but at the expense of the humanities, which were often neglected. Unfortunately, the *científicos* did not think it was necessary to educate the Indians, whom they considered inferior. Only the elite attended the schools. To maintain the peace that the Díaz regime had established, a rural mounted police (*los rurales*) was created. They protected the *hacendados*, holders of large estates (*haciendas*) worked by *peones*, mostly Indians, under a system not unlike that of the Colonial period. The literature—*modernismo*—that flourished during the Díaz dictatorship was entirely divorced from the social problems of the day. The poems and short stories of the *modernistas* did not even hint at the social conditions that prevailed in Mexico at that time. The Realists and Naturalists, although writing novels of social content, were careful not to place any blame on the government.[1] There were, of course, a few exceptions. Heriberto Frías, an army officer, dared to publish a novel, *Tomóchic,* in which he narrates the total destruction of a village in northern Mexico by federal troops. He was court-martialed and sentenced to death for having criticized the government, the official charge being that he had divulged military secrets. Fortunately, he was able to escape the death sentence. Speaking about the novel of the Mexican Revolution, Rulfo said in 1969 that it would not be fair "to omit a reference to a renowned antecedent of the revolutionary novel, *Tomóchic,* by Heriberto Frías, that describes the destruction of a heroic town in Chihuahua by the dictatorship of Porfirio Díaz."[2]

The static society that existed under Díaz came to an end in 1910 with the Revolution initiated by Madero and carried out by the people. Unlike the war for independence fought against Spain one hundred years earlier, Madero's revolution resulted in a complete change of social institutions, attitudes, and manner of living. The Revolution of 1910 catapulted the nation from an almost medieval way of life into the modern age. The country has changed more since that year than during the previous four hundred years. This abrupt change is reflected in the literature produced by the Revolution, a literature entirely different from that of the *modernistas*; a literature that gives a truer picture of the social conditions prevalent during those years, and also of Mexican reality in general. Rulfo has observed that the novels of the Revolution are essentially "direct narratives, sometimes autobiographical memoirs, but always concrete evocations of revolutionary deeds."[3]

With the Revolution Mexico lost its innocence, and with it the apparent happiness which Ramón López Velarde speaks of in his poem "La suave patria" [My beloved country], which ends with these verses:

> My country, I give you the key
> to happiness:
> Be always the same, faithful to
> your daily mirror.
> The fifty beads of the rosary
> are all the same
> And they are happier than you
> my beloved country.[4]

López Velarde died in 1921, the same year he wrote the poem. If the poet were alive today, he would not recognize the Mexico of which he sang because of the tremendous change that has taken place. President Madero's assassination in 1913 resulted in a period of chaos which lasted until 1917. As a consequence of this social upheaval great changes took place. After a new Constitution was adopted in 1917 and the political differences among the leaders were resolved, the country entered upon a period of reconstruction. In his novel *The Trials of a Respectable Family* (1917), Mariano Azuela relates the painful adjustment to the new way of life that a well-to-do family who has lost everything has to undergo to survive. Procopio, the main character, must learn to work with his own hands in order to provide for his pampered wife and children. In still another novel, *Nueva burguesía* (1940), by the same author, the rise of a new middle class who had become the masters of Mexico is vividly portrayed. But the most striking change is found in Azuela's last novel, *Esa sangre* [That blood], in which he returns to the locus of one of his early novels, an *hacienda* in the state of Jalisco, where nothing remains of the old order. The change has been complete.

The Early Years

The world into which Juan Rulfo was born was much like that described by Azuela in *Esa sangre*. The small community where his parents lived and where he was born on 16 May 1918, does not even appear on the maps of the state. Its name is Apulco, and it is located ten miles from Sayula, which has led many critics to believe that he was born there, although it is true that Sayula, which is also the name of the municipality, is the place where his parents registered their son's birth. It is also true that Rulfo did not remain in Apulco more than a few days, for his parents moved to San Gabriel, a town today called Venustiano Carranza, not far from Sayula, which Rulfo uses as the locale for some of his fiction.[5] Rulfo himself said in an interview that took place around 1966 that he was born in "a small village, an agglomeration that belongs to the district of Sayula. Sayula was an important commercial center some years ago, before and even after the Revolution. But I never lived in Sayula. I don't know Sayula. . . . My parents registered me there."[6] The Spanish ancestors of both his father, Juan Nepomuceno Pérez, and his mother, María Vizcaíno Arias, had come to Jalisco (then called Nueva Galicia) during the late eighteenth century. They finally settled in the province of Ávalos (in southern Jalisco) which at that time was a part of New Spain but not of Nueva Galicia. Rulfo has said that his ancestors came to Mexico from northern Spain around 1790.[7] He has given an account of his early ancestry in a colorful prose that is definitely autobiographical:

> My name is Juan Nepomuceno Carlos Pérez Rulfo Vizcaíno. . . . I would have liked a simpler name. My father was called Juan Nepomuceno, my paternal [sic] grandfather was Carlos Vizcaíno; the name Rulfo I have because of Juan del Rulfo, a "caribe" adventurer, so called because he served under José María Calleja, alias "El Caribe," who had a daughter called María Rulfo Navarro, who married my paternal grandfather, José María Jiménez. This Juan del Rulfo arrived in Mexico toward the end of the eighteenth century. . . .[8]

Since Rulfo lived in Apulco such a short time, it is natural that he should consider himself a native of San Gabriel, the town in which he spent his early years and where he attended his first school. There for the first time he heard some of the numerous folk tales of which Mexico is so rich.

> I am a man of Apulco, over there in Jalisco, near Sayula and Zapotlán. I grew up in San Gabriel, and there the people told me many stories: about ghosts, about wars, about crimes. . . . I always lived with country people, people that when the sun goes down light a corn-husk cigarette and suddenly tell whosoever may be near them, "Do you remember?" And even if the listener does not answer, they begin to remember.[9]

This technique of the popular storyteller became the trademark of Rulfo's style.

When Rulfo was two years old the armed aspect of the Mexican Revolution came to an end. In 1920 Álvaro Obregón, conqueror of Francisco Villa at Celaya, came to power, the first post-revolutionary president to last the complete term, which at that time was four years. During that short period Obregón consolidated the gains of his party, the Constitutionalists, and put into effect some of the reforms written into the Constitution of 1917. The Banco de México was created in 1923, the workers began to organize into unions, some states granted voting rights to women, and diplomatic relations with the United States were reestablished. Obregón had named the philosopher José Vasconcelos as his Secretary of Education, and due to his efforts a renaissance in the arts took place. Vasconcelos called upon several painters, among them Diego Rivera and José Clemente Orozco, to decorate the principal government buildings. Their murals, portraying the history of Mexico, had a tremendous influence in the development of a national consciousness. As one critic has said, "the most striking evidence of his [Vasconcelos] contribution to Mexican culture is to be found in the mural movement to which he was midwife in the early 'Twenties."[10] It must not be forgotten, however, that Vasconcelos left behind an extensive body of works on philosophy, as well as several volumes of essays. In reference to his autobiography in four volumes, Rulfo has said:

> The case of José Vasconcelos is different [from that of the novelists of the Revolution]. His series of books initiated with *Ulises criollo,* although autobiographical, is above all the judgment of a thinker of the Revolution. In his work the theoretician, the ideologue of the Revolution, speaks. His works are never a simple narrative; they are a profound inquiry by a man who felt deeply the failure [of the Revolution].[11]

Orozco, one of the two painters called by Vasconcelos to decorate the walls of the government buildings, was born in Zapotlán (now Ciudad Guzmán), not far from Rulfo's birthplace. The world he portrays in his murals is the same that Rulfo was to describe with words thirty years later. The resemblances are striking, especially in the presentation of the characters which reflect, in both artists, the tragic sense of life. In Orozco the tragedy that is Mexican life is the essential characteristic underlying his art; in Rulfo, whose works are limited in number since he has published only three slender volumes, that tragedy is seen only in the Mexico that is the result of social struggle in the countryside, especially during the periods of the Revolution of 1910–17, and the religious war known as the Cristero Revolt, a cruel struggle that sprouted its roots during the presidency of Álvaro Obregón. The Constitution of 1917 which Obregón tried to enforce contained certain restrictions which were considered detrimental to the interests of the church, and the clergy declared itself in open rebellion against the government. They objected mostly to Articles 3 and 27 of the Constitution, the first prohibiting the existence of church-related primary schools, and the second declaring that "religious associations called churches, regardless of their denominations, shall not have the right to acquire, possess, or administer real estate, or have mortgages imposed on them; those who may have them now, either under their name or that of a third party, will be under the jurisdiction of the nation."[12] No less disliked was Article 130, which curtails the rights of priests: their number in each church to be determined by the government; they cannot criticize the laws of the land in public; they shall not have the right to vote, or to form political parties.[13] Rulfo, whose family was greatly affected by the Cristero Revolt, interprets the movement in this manner:

> The revolt of the Cristeros was an internal war that broke out in the states of Colima, Jalisco, Michoacán, Nayarit, Zacatecas, and Guanajuato, against the federal government. There was a decree that enforced an article of the Revolution, according to which priests were forbidden to mix in politics and the churches became the property of the state, as they are today. A set number of priests was assigned to each village, in accordance with its population. Of course, people protested.[14]

Under Plutarco Elías Calles, who had succeeded to the presidency in 1924, the revolt of the Cristeros, fighting under the cry of ¡Viva Cristo Rey!, reached its peak, affecting all families in central Mexico, but principally those in the state of Jalisco. In 1925 Rulfo's father was assassinated, a tragedy that left a profound wound in the young boy. Two years later his mother died of a heart attack. Rulfo remembers those years with these words:

> I went to elementary school in San Gabriel, that is my world. I lived there until I was ten [1928]. It is one of those towns which have lost even their name. Now it is called Venustiano Carranza. There I and my brothers lived with my grandmother—a descendant of the Arias, probably from Andalucía, who had come here in the sixteenth century—until they killed my father.[15]

Some critics have said that his father was killed by a peón; however, Rulfo has denied such an assertion. In his dialogue with the short-story writer Juan José Arreola he clarified that statement by saying, "My father was not killed by a peón. . . . They killed him while he was fleeing . . . and my uncle was also assassinated, and another one, and another one . . . they all died when they were 33."[16]

In 1928 Rulfo was sent to Guadalajara and there he was placed in the Luis Silva School for orphan children. "When the Cristeros ran us out of there," he said, "I arrived in Guadalajara. I was already an orphan. For thirteen pesos a month they registered me in the Orfanatorio Silva, a kind of correctional school."[17] There he remained until 1932, the year he completed his education. Subsequently he registered at the university, but was unable to remain because of a strike. "The strike began," he says, "the same day I entered together with a cousin, a Viscaíno, and lasted about a year and a half. Because of that I went to Mexico City to continue my studying."[18] According to Harss, "that was in 1933, when he was fifteen years old."[19] This, however, could have been in early 1934.[20]

The City on the Lake

The Cristero Revolt ended in 1928, the last year of the presidency of Plutarco Elías Calles and also the year that Obregón, who had been reelected, was assassinated. That precipitated a great deal of turmoil, dominated by the struggle for political power among the different revolutionary factions. Emilio Portes Gil ruled as provisional president until the duly elected candidate, Pascual Ortiz Rubio, took office in December 1929. The opposition candidate, José Vasconcelos, declared that the election had been fraudulent and left the country, fearing for his life. Ortiz Rubio, under pressure, was forced to resign in 1932, and Abelardo Rodríguez took over as provisional president until the elections of 1933, when Lázaro Cárdenas was elected for the period 1934–1940.

During these unsettled years Rulfo, desiring to continue his education, attended the National University for a short time, with the financial help of his uncle. But before long his relative, claiming economic difficulties, stopped the meager help, and Rulfo had to abandon the university and seek employment. Apparently there were other reasons for having discontinued his studies. He has said that he was "supposed to study law," for his grandfather had been a lawyer, "and someone had to use his books. But much time had passed, and I had forgotten a great deal. I was unable to pass the qualifying exam to which we were submitted. Thus I had to go to work. I left school because I was not interested in the study of law."[21]

Rulfo's uncle advised him to change his name to Juan Pérez, which was more in keeping with his economic condition. However, Juan disregarded the advice and continued to use his paternal grandmother's name. Those were difficult times for Rulfo, who by now had decided to become a writer. Luckily, the young man was able to obtain a government position in 1935, where he was to remain for ten years.[22] Of this period of his life he says, "I began to work as an immigration agent with the Department of the Interior. Yes, I caught undesirable foreigners. First here, in Mexico City, and then in Tampico, and all over the country. I went to Guadalajara once more."[23]

Under the governments of Lázaro Cárdenas (1934–1940) and Manuel Ávila Camacho (1940–1946), great transformations took place in the life of the nation, and for Rulfo himself. Beginning in December 1940 Ávila Camacho changed the course that Mexico had been following under the leadership of Cárdenas by stopping all social reforms and by emphasizing the importance of industrialization. The social revolution had come to an end, and with it a period in which interest in national problems, such as the future of the Indian, land reform, and oil expropriation, was reflected in the literature and the arts. Rulfo, besides having to adjust to life in the capital, had to work to support himself, in addition to finding time for his writing. He first intended to write a novel, of which little is known besides the title, "El hijo del desaliento" [Son of affliction], and a short fragment dated 1940 entitled "Un pedazo de noche" [A night's fragment]. Much has been made of the novel's title, often given as "El hijo del desconsuelo" [Son of dejection].[24] Critics assume, because of the title and because of Rulfo's precarious situation during those years, that it was autobiographical, and that it foreshadows some of the situations that are found in his later novel, *Pedro Páramo*.[25] Rulfo himself has said about his novel:

I had to be a writer. The novel which I wrote soon after I arrived in Mexico City, dealing with solitude and things like that, was written in third person; it contained biographical materials, events that had actually happened to me, but applied to another personage. . . . But I did not like it. I don't think I saved any of it. It seems that a periodical, many years ago, published a fragment, as a short story. As for the rest, I threw it away. It was a rather conventional novel, very highstrung, in which I tried to express certain solitary feelings.[26]

At Immigration, Rulfo's coworker Efrén Hernández, already famous as a short-story writer, taught him the art of prose writing, especially that of the short story. And it was he also, as a friend of Marco Antonio Millán, editor of the periodical *América,* who was instrumental in getting some of Rulfo's best stories published. Here is how Millán remembers those days:

Having established relations with Efrén Hernández and Margarita [Michelena], Juan Rulfo came to our meetings, having been presented by Hernández as a first-rate short-story writer. . . . Juan's prestige grew as we published little by little almost all of the stories of *El llano en llamas*—years later edited by the Fondo de Cultura Económica; but it was with us that he began to be appreciated by other writers.[27]

In 1945, the year that *América* published his first story, "La vida no es muy seria en sus cosas" [Life is not very serious about things], Rulfo, in Guadalajara, joined Juan José Arreola and Antonio Alatorre in the publication of the literary periodical *Pan,* where his stories "Macario" and "Nos han dado la tierra" [They have given us the land] appeared that same year.

During the Second World War Mexico's industrialization continued unabated. Initiated by Ávila Camacho, it continued under the presidencies of Miguel Alemán (1947–1952) and Adolfo Ruiz Cortines (1953–1958), the former remembered as the builder of University City in the Pedregal, and the latter for having granted women the right to vote, in 1955. During these years Rulfo had left his position at the Immigration Service (in 1947) to go to work for a private company, F. G. Goodrich, where he was assigned to the Department of Sales. In 1948 he married. He was to remain at Goodrich until 1954.[28]

With the help of a fellowship from the Centro Mexicano de Escritores received in 1952, Rulfo had more leisure time to dedicate to writing and also decided to collect the stories already published, added a few more, and offered the book to the prestigious Fondo de Cultura Económica, the semi-official publishing house in Mexico City. The book, his first, appeared in 1953 with the title *El llano en llamas* [The burning plain]. It was an immediate success. His Centro fellowship was extended for 1953 and 1954, and it is assumed that it was during those years that he began to write the novel *Pedro Páramo,* although he may have had some of it already written before that time. The fact is that in 1954 he published a chapter from it in the periodicals *Las Letras Patrias, Dintel,* and *Revista de la Universidad de México.*

The year 1955 was an eventful one for Rulfo. Besides publishing his first novel, he accepted a position with the government which, under the leadership of President Alemán, had begun the development of the Papaloapan River basin in southern Mexico. The project was discontinued in 1956, and Rulfo went back to Mexico City. In 1958 he again returned to office work, having accepted a position in the Library of the Sociedad Mexicana de Geografía y Estadística, a government-supported institution.

Guadalajara Interlude

Although Rulfo had attained world recognition as one of Mexico's outstanding prose writers, he had not yet been able to solve his personal problems. In 1959 he decided to take his family to Guadalajara in search not only of a better economic status, but also of peace and tranquillity.

However, he was not able to find in Guadalajara (on Oñate Street) what he so much desired, for the city at that time was being transformed into a large and noisy metropolis with most of the inconveniences of Mexico City, but without its rewards. Things took a turn for the worse, complicated by his excessive drinking and ill health.

While in Guadalajara Rulfo was associated with Televicentro, the state-sponsored television station, where he was in charge of publicity. The station is located in the Casa de la Cultura, part of a community center in Parque Agua Azul, and offers all types of cultural and artistic programs. Rulfo participated in some of these activities, often contributing with write-ups or program notes like that which he dedicated to the painter Jorge Hurtado.[29] At the same time he wrote another novel, "El gallero" [The cockfighter], which was not published. However, the narrative was used in the motion picture *El gallo de oro* [The golden cock], whose script was prepared by Carlos Fuentes and Gabriel García Márquez, two now-famous novelists. The film was released in 1964. At the same time Rulfo was broadening his activities through another medium of expression, photography, which became a lifetime hobby and has resulted in the publication of some photographs in magazines. In his last book, *El gallo de oro,* he included a sequence of four photographs entitled "Los músicos." In the same year, the National Institute of Fine Arts published a book containing one hundred of his photographs.[30]

Another activity undertaken by Rulfo during these years in Guadalajara was the editing of history books. This is the way he explains his interest in the history of his native state:

The thing is, in Guadalajara . . . the Industrial Bank of Jalisco . . . publishes a history book every year as a gift to its clients. So I had an idea: to try to incorporate the whole history of Jalisco from the days of the early chronicles, and bring it out regularly, once a year, as before, in book form. To make up for the poison people were being fed on television, they'd be given a book.[31]

This grandiose idea was hardly realized. But he did edit a volume relating to the early history of Jalisco which he published in 1959 with an Introduction. The book, *Noticias históricas de la vida y hechos de Nuño de Guzmán,* deals with the life and deeds of the conquistador of Jalisco (then called Nueva Galicia), Nuño de Guzmán, a fierce lieutenant in the army of Hernán Cortés whose conquest of Central Mexico in 1529 was marked by cruelty toward the Indians. In 1531 he founded Guadalajara, giving the city the name of his birthplace in Castile.

While Rulfo was busy in the archives of Guadalajara investigating the history of Jalisco, his name was becoming popular outside Mexico through the translation of his novel *Pedro Páramo*. The first translation into a European language was done by Mariana Frenck, who published the German version in Munich in 1958. The American translation first appeared in 1959, done by Lysander Kemp, who was living in Guadalajara during those years and was acquainted with Rulfo. Published under the same title by Grove Press, it made the name of Rulfo known among American readers. In the same year the novel was translated into French by Roger Lescot; in 1960 it appeared in Sweden, in 1961 in Denmark and Norway, in 1962 in Italy and Holland, and later in other countries. His collection of short stories, *El llano en llamas,* was also receiving attention in Europe and the United States, although the translations were not as numerous as those of *Pedro Páramo*. However, some of the individual stories appeared in English as early as 1955, the first being "Anacleto Morones," translated by Irene Nicholson under the title "The Miraculous Child," and published in the September issue of *Encounter*. The first translation of the complete collection of stories into a foreign language was that of Giuseppe Cintioli in Italian with the title *La morte al Messico* in 1963.[32]

Stability in Mexico City

The year Rulfo went to Guadalajara was the first year of the presidency of Adolfo López Mateos (1959–1964), a period characterized by the great effort that was made on the part of the government to achieve a higher level of industrialization and a higher standard of living. Agriculture, however, was overlooked, and the rural population moved in ever-increasing numbers to the cities. By that time the Revolution had been completely institutionalized and the main preoccupation of the people was upward mobility. These changes in Mexican society were dramatically described by Carlos Fuentes in his novels *Where the Air Is Clear* (1958) and *The Death of Artemio Cruz* (1962).

Rulfo, unhappy and disillusioned in Guadalajara, decided in spite of his ill health to go back once more to Mexico City. He arrived in the thriving capital in 1962 and went to work at the Instituto Nacional Indigenista, a government institution created in 1948 and directed since that year, and until his death in 1970, by the world-famous archaeologist and anthropologist Alfonso Caso. The purpose of the Institute is to study the

problems of the native population of Mexico, to propose to the government the measures necessary to solve these problems, and to see that once
those measures are approved, they are implemented. Rulfo's activities at
the Institute today deal with all three functions, and naturally he is kept
extremely busy, since he is also in charge of editing the Institute's
magazine *México Indígena*. At the same time, he has engaged in the
writing of scripts for experimental, commercial films. It is ironic that the
adaptation of his own novel, *Pedro Páramo*, was not done by himself. The
film, based on his novel and released in 1966, was done by Carlos Fuentes
and Carlos Velo. Rulfo was not pleased with it, having said that they had
turned his novel into a western.

   Although his work at the Institute left Rulfo little time to write, he
nevertheless undertook the writing of a new novel, to be called "La
cordillera" [The packtrain], a book that has never been published. As early
as 1963, however, he described to a reporter from the newspaper *Excélsior*
the nature of the novel, saying that it had to do with the history of a town,
Ejutla, important during the Colonial period and the nineteenth century
because it was a transfer point for the travelers who used the *cordillera* to go
from the North and the Pacific Coast to Central Mexico. The town in the
story, like that in *Pedro Páramo*, was to be brought to life through the
experiences of a family. In 1964, in another interview, this time published
in *La Gaceta* of the Fondo de Cultura Económica, Rulfo added more
details, stating that the novel is about a family founded in the southern
part of the state of Jalisco during the sixteenth century by Dionisio Arias
Pinzón, a Spanish *encomendero* from Vizcay. The family disintegrates over
the years and at the time of the Revolution the only descendants left are
Diego Arias and his grandmother Tránsito Pinzón, isolated from the world
and with nothing left but their solitude. According to this version, the
town is called Ayuquila, and not Ejutla.[33]
   In 1965, in a public dialogue with Juan José Arreola held in the Sala
Manuel Ponce of Bellas Artes in Mexico City, Rulfo gave an excuse for not
having finished the novel. He said, "I am not a professional writer. . . . I
write when I feel like it . . . that is why I have not finished *La cordillera*
. . . and not because of success, fear, or any of those things they are
saying. . . ."[34] The following year, according to Harss, he was still
engaged in polishing the novel: "He is trying to bring himself to release an
eternally forthcoming novel he has finished and torn apart a thousand
times, called *La cordillera.*"[35] Although the novel has not been published
to date, very brief excerpts from it appeared in the periodical *Siempre!* in
1966. Nevertheless, some critics have stated in writing that the novel was

published in 1965 or 1966, even elaborating upon its content and style.[36] It seems, however, that by 1968 Rulfo had already stopped revising the manuscript and had given up the idea of finishing the novel. Instead, he spoke about publishing another collection of short stories. To the question, "Could you tell us when we are going to see in the bookstores the book *La cordillera* that you have announced?" Rulfo answered, "Well, that book was a novel on which I was working, but I have stopped it. Now I am writing a series of stories to publish at the end of the year [1968] that I shall call 'Días sin floresta' [Barren days]."[37]

All of the above statements indicate that Rulfo has been actively writing, although he does not feel obligated to publish, a right he has strongly defended. He has, since May 1964, been a member of the Editorial Board of the monthly periodical *El cuento,* dedicated to the publishing of international short stories. He himself edits a section called "Retenes" [Clippings] in which he publishes selections from well-known writers on diverse topics. These selections are important since they reflect his literary interests.

Even though Rulfo has published only three books, he has attained greater international renown than many prolific writers. This fact was recognized by the Mexican government in 1970 when it bestowed upon Rulfo the Premio Nacional de Letras, worth 300,000 pesos. Agustín Yáñez, author of the famous novel *Al filo del agua* [At the edge of the storm] and at that time President of the Mexican Academy of Letters, presented the prize and read a few remarks about Rulfo's works. Among other things he said:

Two brief [but] substantial, deeply Mexican, strongly provincial books have been enough to give Juan Rulfo and Mexico a universal dimension, since these books by this inspired writer have reached the largest number of translations into different languages. This proves the indisputable thesis that universality is only obtained by probing deeply into the essence of what is national. . . . Rulfo transforms colloquial language and gives it an aesthetic category. . . . This has been his triumph; this his path of magical realism open to the future of our letters, of our authentic expression, comparable only to that of our great painters. . . .[38]

In 1980 his importance as a writer was recognized by the Academia Mexicana de la Lengua. In September he became a member, occupying the chair held by the famous poet José Gorostiza, about whom Rulfo spoke in his acceptance speech.[39] Other organizations such as the Instituto Nacional de Bellas Artes held conferences in his honor. In that same year his novelette, *El gallo de oro,* was also published.

Just as Rulfo received help from Efrén Hernández in his early struggle to become a writer, so he now helps other young aspiring writers at the Centro Mexicano de Escritores in his capacity as one of the directors, with Francisco Monterde and Salvador Elizondo.

On meeting Rulfo—lean, of average height, light complexion, and a heavy smoker—one gets the impression of an anguished man. His lined face reveals years of physical and spiritual suffering. Although he avoids crowds and company in general, when he is with friends he is frank, quite talkative, and not at all reserved, speaking slowly and in a low, soft voice. In his conversation he never speaks condescendingly of writers, and his main topics of conversation are literature, history, and Mexican Indian cultures. As one of his many interviewers has said, "What he knows about his country is very impressive, about pre-Hispanic cultures, the colonial period, the nineteenth century. Scores of names of native peoples and tribes come forth in his conversation without the least of scholarly pretensions, only with the purpose of illustrating this or that statement."[40]

Rulfo is extremely well read, being acquainted with the literatures of several European and American countries. His favorite authors are, of course, novelists, especially the Russians, Scandinavians, Italians, Americans, and Brazilians. His interest in literature, and above all fiction, dates back to his early years in San Gabriel. The local priest had left his grandmother a small library which Rulfo utilized to advantage. The first novels read were those of Salgari and Dumas, books of adventure liked by most boys. Then he became interested in English, American, and northern European novelists. The novel *Hunger* by Knut Hamsun, read while still a boy, left a deep impression on him, since he could identify with the characters. "How could he forget it?" asks Hellén Ferro, "He well knew the meaning of the word when he read that novel."[41] Later he went on to read more sophisticated novels by Joyce, Faulkner, Woolf, Dos Passos, Hemingway, Björnson, Halldór Laxness, C. F. Ramuz, Lagerlöff, Sillanpää, Andreyev, and Korolenko. Among the contemporary French writers one of his favorites is Jean Giono; among the Germans, Günter Grass, and among the Italians Vasco Pratolini. In 1965 Rulfo gave a lecture on the contemporary novel in which he expressed his opinions about these and other novelists. It is a lecture that reflects a great knowledge of the novel, and an excellent taste.[42] In his interview with Elena Poniatowska Rulfo said, "Before, I heard many voices, and still hear them . . . Marcel Proust, William Faulkner, Virginia Woolf, Knut

Hamsun, and what have you . . . the Bible and Prudentius' hymns. To be sure, my first great book, the one that opened my eyes, was James Joyce's *The Young Man as an Artist* [*sic*]. . . ."[43] But most of all he admires Halldór Laxness. When asked the question, "What book from universal literature would you have liked to write?" he answered, "*Salka Valka* by Halldör Laxness."[44]

Rulfo's knowledge of the Mexican novel is also extensive. In 1969 he addressed himself to the subject, expressing, as always, his frank opinions. For him, the great Mexican novel begins with the Revolution; before that the novel had really not obtained its independence from Spain. Of the novels of the Revolution he praises *Tomóchic* (a prerevolutionary novel by Heriberto Frías), Azuela's *Los de abajo* [The underdogs], Rafael Muñoz's *Se llevaron el cañón para Bachimba* [They took the cannon to Bachimba], Gregorio López y Fuentes's *Campamento* [Army camp], Martín Luis Guzmán's *La sombra del caudillo* [The dictator's shadow] and *El águila y la serpiente* [The Eagle and the Serpent], and Cipriano Campos Alatorre's *Los fusilados* [The executed], the latter a little-known novel that has a great resemblance to Rulfo's own works. Of his contemporaries he has praised Agustín Yáñez (whose *At the Edge of the Storm* he considers to be the culmination of the novel of the Revolution), Vicente Leñero, Carlos Fuentes, Salvador Elizondo, Fernando del Paso, Rosario Castellanos, and Elena Garro. Of the younger generation he tells us only that the most talented are those writing in the publication *Punto de Partida*.[45]

The question most often asked Rulfo concerns his future publications. There is no doubt that since 1955 he has written other novels and short stories, although they remain unpublished. To several interviewers he has said, "Contrary to what some think, I have never stopped writing. I have stopped publishing, but I shall never stop writing."[46]

Chapter Two
First Prose Writings
Introduction

Juan Rulfo has acknowledged his indebtedness to Efrén Hernández for having taught him the craft of short-story writing. In the development of this genre in Mexico, Hernández represents the transition between the writers who were active during the upheaval of the Mexican Revolution (1910–1940) and those of the post–World War II generation. This change has been one of the most significant in the development of contemporary Mexican letters.

Although best known for their novels, the fiction writers of the Mexican Revolution gave a great deal of attention to the short story. It seems that those agitated times produced a narrative that is characterized by its fragmentary nature. Even the novels of this period tend to be episodic; and sometimes, as with Martín Luis Guzmán's *El águila y la serpiente* (1928), it is difficult to determine if the work is a novel or a collection of stories united by an overall historical frame of reference, the Mexican Revolution.

Like the novel, the short story of the Revolution is the product of social events that began in 1910 and ended in the late thirties—the great change that took place as a result of the struggle against the dictator Porfirio Díaz; the counterrevolution led by Victoriano Huerta; and the religious war of the late 1920s known as the Cristero Revolt, precipitated when the government tried to put into effect the Constitution of 1917. One of the results of the Revolution was the desire on the part of Mexican writers to divorce themselves from the past and to reshape the image of Mexico. This they accomplished by creating a new literary language and adopting new attitudes toward reality, society, and the individual. The rigid social class distinctions which were reflected in the spoken and written language inherited from the Colonial period were crumbling. The creation of a new image of Mexico was due in great part to the efforts of the mural painters (Diego Rivera, José Clemente Orozco, David Alfaro Siqueiros) and the novelists of the period, especially Mariano Azuela, Martín Luis Guzmán, Rafael Muñoz, Gregorio López y Fuentes, Francisco Rojas González, and Cipriano Campos Alatorre. These writers are also the creators of the short story of the Mexican Revolution, whose subject matter is not only the armed conflict, but also the social changes that took place. Its form, for the first time, is not copied from European or North American models; it is original, the result of authors writing under pressure, sometimes while on the march with the armies or even, like Azuela, while the fighting was going on. They gave expression to a subject matter that was close at hand, since most of the writers had been active revolutionaries. For this reason their prose often resembles that of the wartime reporter. Their originality also comes from the fact that they were not writing for the elite, as were the *modernistas,* but for the new social classes created by the Revolution. The desire to communicate immediately their experiences prevented them from taking time out to revise and polish their prose style. That was to come later with Guzmán, Revueltas, Yáñez, and Rulfo. The number of writers multiplied, many of them with little previous training in the art of the short story, but with a great desire to tell of their experiences in the form of semifictional reports. Thus their stories often made use of an open form, where historical fact and fictitious invention blend to give the impression of a chronicle. The line between history and fiction becomes blurred in the short story of the Mexican Revolution.[1]

Although Rulfo was born when the Revolution was in progress, he was old enough during the Cristero Revolt to have experienced its consequences. The Revolution forms the background of his novel, *Pedro Páramo,* and some of the stories from *El llano en llamas.* He could not be classified as a short-story writer of the Revolution, however, since his technique, style, and tone are different. Nevertheless, some of his stories, like "El llano en llamas," have much in common with the stories by writers of the previous generation.

If a comparison is made between Rulfo's best-known story of the Revolution, "El llano en llamas," and Francisco Rojas González's earlier story "El caso de Pancho Planas" (1934), the similarities as well as the differences come to light. Both protagonists, *El Pichón* and Pancho Planas, are common soldiers who have experienced fighting. While Rojas González tells the story of Pancho from his own point of view, Rulfo allows *El Pichón* to relate his own. Rojas González, although very sympathetic to Pancho's plight, looks at him from a superior point of reference. His own interpretation of events interrupts Pancho's story about his unsuccessful desire to become a sergeant. His characterization of Pancho is made according to traditional techniques; that is, presenting a portrait of the character in the introduction before any action takes place. Rulfo's story, as told by *El Pichón,* begins in the midst of the action, a battle between federal soldiers and revolutionaries. Much more important is Rulfo's technique in integrating the telling of the story with the description of the ambience. In Rojas González's story, the description of the railroad car in which the narrator meets Pancho and hears his story is given little importance. Pancho's story unfolds the historical sequence of the Revolution; that of *El Pichón* concentrates on a single event, the part that a minor revolutionary played in that same Revolution. Perhaps the most important difference between Rulfo and the short-story writers of the Revolution is his complete detachment from the world he creates. Earlier writers were unable to see the Revolution with detachment as they were too close to it. However, in this particular story, Rulfo betrays some influence of the writers of the Revolution, especially that of Mariano Azuela.[2]

The Avant-garde Short Story

The literature of the Mexican Revolution was really an eruption that prevailed for only three decades. Its social content, vigor, and originality helped it triumph over the other literary trend represented by the members of the avant-garde movement, of European origin. These writers were the direct descendants of the postmodernists—Alfonso Reyes, Julio Torri, and Artemio del Valle Arizpe—prose writers who had introduced the fantastic and the archaeological short story. Their influence was decisive in the formation of the style of the avant-garde writers, represented by Jaime Torres Bodet, Xavier Villaurrutia, Salvador Novo, and Gilberto Owen. This group, known as the *Contemporáneos* (title of the periodical they published during the 1930s), introduced into the Mexican short story new techniques and at the same time revitalized the style. However, their main preoccupation was poetry, and they did not give the short story the attention it deserved. It is for this reason that there are no outstanding *cuentistas* among them.

A short story similar to that written by the *Contemporáneos* was being produced at the time by writers not associated directly with the group. The stories of José Martínez Sotomayor, Efrén Hernández, and Agustín Yáñez, written in a highly polished style and treating of intranscendental themes, had a decided influence upon the writers of the following generation, among them Juan Rulfo. Of the three, Hernández was perhaps the most influential. Although he had published his first story, "Tachas" (with an Introduction by Salvador Novo), in 1928, and four more in 1932 under the title of one of them, *El señor de palo,* it was not until 1941, when the National University of Mexico published his *Cuentos,* a collection of nine stories, that Hernández's influence among young writers became widespread. Four years later Rulfo began to publish his own stories, first in the periodical *América,* one of whose editors was Hernández.

Hernández's book marks a definite break with the past. In his stories the anecdote is no longer the most important aspect of the story. He skillfully subordinates it and brings out other narrative elements. This shift in interest from anecdote to less important aspects of the story, such as the sheer pleasure of describing the atmosphere (as Rulfo does in his story "Luvina"), or the introduction of inconsequential motifs, became one of the characteristics of the new short story, as practiced by Juan José Arreola, Augusto Monterroso, and others. The heavy, melodramatic elements of the previous realistic stories gave way to a light, entertaining, urbane literature that captured the attention of young writers. Rulfo was to apply this technique to the treatment of tragic elements and produce the most original stories of the twentieth century by a Mexican writer.

The New Short Story

During the early 1940s an interest in creating a new literature was evident among such writers as Octavio Paz and José Revueltas. As a result of World War II, Mexico began to industrialize, with a consequent shift in political attitudes. The revolutionary leaders were now more interested in creating material wealth for the people than in radical social reforms. The abandonment of the principles of the Revolution led to disillusionment on the part of the intellectuals. That frustration is evident in the essays of Octavio Paz and the fiction of José Revueltas, author of the collection of stories *Dios en la tierra* (1944).

Revueltas, as did Rulfo in *El llano en llamas,* combined elements present in the stories of his precursors. He also drew upon techniques perfected by Anglo-American writers. For his subject matter he went back to the social writers of the Mexican Revolution; for his style he utilized the lessons taught by the *Contemporáneos*; and for his narrative technique he relied upon William Faulkner and other fiction writers of the United States. This influence by Faulkner has been denied by both Revueltas and Rulfo. "Revueltas and I," Rulfo has said, "are regularly attributed Faulkner's influence. Revueltas denies it and it's the same case with me. Revueltas wrote his works before becoming acquainted with that author. I did not know him either but became acquainted with him *a posteriori* to see where the resemblance was."[3] Needless to say, the fact remains that both wrote short stories of dramatic intensity which were, at the same time, experimental, like those of Faulkner. The influence of Revueltas upon Rulfo and his generation and upon even younger writers has been most noticeable. The new short story in Mexico cannot be satisfactorily explained without considering his contribution to its development. Revueltas, without abandoning native subject matter, tried to solve the problems of narrative technique. He may have failed somewhat in that he was, unlike Rulfo, too explicit in his editorializing. But his lessons did not go unheeded, for soon after there appeared such famous short-story writers as Juan José Arreola, Juan Rulfo, and Carlos Fuentes.

The short stories of Arreola and Rulfo, who were born only a few months apart in the same region of Jalisco, cannot be compared since they belong to two different modes of fiction, the ironic and the tragic. Arreola's *Confabulario* (1952, but written during the 1940s) is made up of fantastic and ironical stories, some of which mock the most respected ideas and institutions of contemporary man. In others Arreola elaborates classical parables or re-creates the lives of famous men of antiquity. In Rulfo's stories, on the other hand, not a single allusion to literature is to be found, and historical references are at a minimum.[4] His material is derived from the countryside; his personages are *campesinos*; his tone is somber and tragic. The comparison that Emmanuel Carballo drew between Arreola and Rulfo soon after the appearance of *El llano en llamas* is still valid today:

> Arreola universalizes his experiences, while Rulfo introduces, deforming them, personal reminiscenses into his collective subject matter. Arreola proposes problems that could occur anywhere, while Rulfo, starting from a localized place and digging deeply, gives what is national, and even regional, a universal tone. Arreola is a fabulist in most of his works, while Rulfo limits himself, in all of his, to the presentation of personages and situations bereft of an ulterior moral lesson. . . . Arreola presents subtle moral cases and imbricated intellectual problems. Rulfo, on the contrary, deals in depth with problems related to daily life.[5]

Nevertheless, Rulfo and Arreola complement each other in that they present two faces of Mexican literature, the popular and the erudite, the national and the cosmopolitan. Both opened new avenues for the younger writers, among them Carlos Fuentes, who has, since the 1950s, become the most important fiction writer in Mexico. His first book, *Días enmascarados* (1954), is a collection of six short stories in which he was able to combine elements derived from Arreola and Rulfo and yet create a different type of short story that was neither *arreolesque* (fantastic or satirical) nor *rulfesque* (neorealistic or of magic realism), but a synthesis of the two with which he was able to erase the duality between the national and the cosmopolitan, as represented by Rulfo and Arreola.

Rulfo's First Story: "Un pedazo de noche"

In 1953 Juan Rulfo published his first book, *El llano en llamas* [The burning plain], an immediate success. Overnight Rulfo became famous as a short-story writer who represented the national trend. Yet, his style and technique were sophisticated enough for him to be considered not only the last of the short story writers of the Revolution, but also a pioneer of the new literature that was being written throughout Latin America. As soon as the book was published, critics began to search for other prose writings by Rulfo. To their surprise they discovered that he had published only a handful of stories in obscure periodicals. Most of these stories were collected in *The Burning Plain*. He did, however, omit one of them, "La vida no es muy seria en sus cosas" [Life is not very serious about things], which had appeared in 1945.[6] Another short fragment not included (apparently his earliest prose writing) appeared in 1959 in the *Revista de Literatura Mexicana* in Mexico City. It is dated January 1940 and has the title "Un pedazo de noche" [A night's fragment]. These stories remained hidden until recently, when they were both included in his *Antología personal* (1978).

Although "Un pedazo de noche" seems to be a chapter of a longer work, it has the structure of a short story.[7] Since it remained unpublished until 1959, it is difficult to determine if any modifications were made to the 1940 original. The story is told by the protagonist, a prostitute of the red-light district. Her name, Olga or Pilar, is of no importance to her. "It is all the same, one name or another. What is a name good for?"[8] Although the story is seen from the perspective of the girl, it is really about the gravedigger Claudio Marcos, whose solitude drives him to search for companionship. When he approaches Pilar he is carrying a baby belonging to his *comadre* Flaviana, who went off with her drunken husband. Pilar asks Claudio if he takes advantage of his *comadre* when her husband is drunk, but he says no, because the two of them get drunk together and they are always together everywhere, "hasta que se les cae o se les pierde la memoria" ("until they can't remember a thing"). Taking care of the abandoned baby assuages Claudio's loneliness and desire for a family. He finally marries Pilar, but is still left alone at home while she continues in her old ways. He finds consolation in burying people. "Dead people," he says, "bother no one; but the living, they can't find enough ways to make life miserable for others" (149). Claudio's tragedy lies in the overwhelming love that he has for others; Pilar's is caused by her prisonlike life of prostitution. She lives in constant fear of the sadistic "nut-cracker," the man who lords over the women of Trujano Street.

This early story reflects traces of style and technique that are later to predominate in Rulfo's writings. One of the characteristics of his style, already present here, is the aura of vagueness that hovers over the identification of people and things and the indecisiveness of the characters. For example, when Claudio approaches Pilar with the baby in his arms and asks her how much she charges, she says, "No . . . not with that thing you're carrying" (144). After walking with Claudio in search of a room, they stop to eat. Pilar refers to Claudio as "aquel fulano" ("that guy"). "Already there, among so many people, smelling the strong odor of the frying *chorizo,* I even forgot what I was doing with that guy sitting in front of me" (147). And even after he tells her his name, she refers to him as "the one who presumably was called Claudio Marcos" (148). Often a sense of mystery is introduced by not identifying the characters. The man in charge of the prostitutes is always referred to as "the man who cracks the nuts." When Pilar first arrives at Trujano Street the girls tell her that in order to obtain a place on that street she must first have her nut cracked. Pilar comments, "I do not want to reveal what that act consisted of, because even if not a trace of shame is left on me, there is something inside me that seeks to forget the bad memories" (143).

Also present in this early story is the stylistic device of personifying the emotions, which Rulfo was later to bring to a high degree of perfection. Talking about her fear, Pilar thinks: "And although on many occasions I felt its tremors, he [fear] tried to hide when he saw my needs, perhaps and surely for fear of my sending him away to live alone, because fear is the thing that fears solitude the most, according to what I know" (143–44). No less conspicuous in this "fragment" is Rulfo's keenness in characterization. Unlike his predecessors, he removes himself completely from the scene and allows his personages to characterize themselves. Action, circumstance, and dialogue are the devices used. Pilar does not need to tell her profession; it is revealed at the beginning by the name of the street where she works, a well-known red-light district. A little later she is more explicit: "One night a man approached me. That was not important, for that is why I was there, to be sought by men" (144). With Claudio, Rulfo uses dialogue. Step by step, as Claudio reveals his life to Pilar, the reader becomes acquainted with the gravedigger. Even the baby in his arms becomes a person. He is characterized by references made by both Claudio and Pilar during that journey in the night. Gradually, although he never speaks, the baby comes to life. First Pilar refers to him as "eso que llevas encima" ("that thing you are carrying"). A little later he becomes a "criatura." Soon after, Pilar says,

"I kept looking at the baby, who kept on squirming in his arms. His eyes were those of grown-up people, full of malice and bad intentions. He seemed to be the reflection of our vices . . . I was thinking of that when the little boy's eyes began to smile. He extended his arms and jumped and laughed with me, showing me his only tooth. . . . I held him against my neck patting him on the back so he would go to sleep. But that baby was not sleepy; he squirmed like a worm and searched with his mouth there where he knew that the food was." (145).

In the presentation of the story Rulfo already makes use of certain narrative techniques that are to become his trademark. The first-person narrator tells the story in the present about an incident which occurred long ago and which she is remembering, but she relates it as if it had just happened or was then happening. The story begins with the words "Someone told me there was an empty space on Valerio Trujano Lane . . ." and continues, "I was then just a beginner" (143). That statement brings the reader to an indefinite past, the time when Pilar first met Claudio. However, the dialogue is presented as if the action were taking place in the present. The first part of the story ends with Pilar conscious of Claudio sitting at the foot of the bed. In the second part, which is very short, the narrator brings the reader to the present, the time when the story is being told, by beginning with the words, "It was the same person now sitting on the edge of my bed. . . ." This device, which abolishes time, making past and present one, was to become one of the essential elements in the narrative technique of Juan Rulfo.

"La vida no es muy seria en sus cosas"

The story "La vida no es muy seria en sus cosas" [Life is not very serious about things] displays a more elementary technique of storytelling and a less-sophisticated subject matter, although no less original and not less tragic, than later stories or even the one published that same year, "They Gave Us the Land." It deals with the experiences of an expectant mother who has lost her husband and has therefore put all her hopes of happiness on her future son, whom she already calls Crispín, after the dead father, for she is sure the child will be a boy. Her entire life fluctuates between two emotions, her grief over losing her husband and the hope of soon having a son to replace him. However, her concern for her dead husband leads her to a second tragedy, the loss of her future son. Wishing to visit the cemetery, she looks for a coat on the upper shelf of a closet so that she can shield her unborn child from the cold. She falls and, it is suggested, has a miscarriage, or perhaps dies.

Even with such a melodramatic subject matter, Rulfo is able to avoid mawkishness by controlling the sentiments expressed by the mother when thinking about her dead husband, and by eliminating a detailed description of her fall and its consequences, which are only suggested: "Something pushed her. Below, the floor was very far, out of reach. . . ."[9] Already there appears in this first story Rulfo's preoccupation with death. The protagonist is conscious of death's presence, since death has already taken her husband and could very well take her unborn son. She visualizes death as "a slowly swelling river pushing the old waters and covering them slowly, never rushing like a young stream would do" (155). That is the way she imagines death to be, for she has seen death more than once and therefore knows that death can do whatever it wants, especially to those who are unaware of it.

The relationship between the mother and her unborn child gives substance to the story. The young girl consoles herself with the knowledge that she will soon have a son, but she is still too emotionally involved with the memory of her dead husband to be entirely conscious of the existence of the baby. Her mood is often interrupted when the baby kicks her, as she explains it, to manifest his jealousy. The omniscient narrator interprets the feelings and sentiments of the eight-month-old baby. The story opens with a description of Crispín inside the womb, so the narrator must use his imagination to present what cannot be seen: "Crispín was unaware of this [his mother's thoughts]. He only moved a little, when he felt the vacuum that his mother's sighs caused on one of the sides. On the other hand, it even seemed that the sighs let him be better accommodated, so that he could continue to sleep, lulled by the sound of the blood on its steady and repeated flow up and down, hour after hour" (155).

The story, which has been rejected by Rulfo as unworthy of his ability, has merit, and it can only be considered inferior when compared with his later stories. It is not as rich in stylistic devices as "A Night's Fragment"; nevertheless, the preoccupation with death, the communication of the mother with the unborn child, and the interpretation of the child's feelings are elements that soon were to be transformed into richer fiction. The element of irony in the story—the mother's tragedy as the result of her preoccupation with the life of her future son—is to reappear in some of the short stories of *The Burning Plain* as well as in the novel *Pedro Páramo*. Donald K. Gordon says, "'La vida no es muy seria en sus cosas' is an excellent example of displaced love." He also observes that the mother foreshadows a character in *Pedro Páramo*, Dorotea, whose great desire is to have a child. "The desperate desire to be a mother, which at the end is frustrated, is the same."[10]

Chapter Three
The Burning Plain:
The Early Stories

Introduction

Although Rulfo was busy writing in the late 1930s and early 1940s, nothing remains of that early period except the fragment "Un pedazo de noche" (1940). In 1945, however, three and perhaps four of his stories appeared in the reviews *Pan* of Guadalajara, *América* of Mexico City, and some others.[1] "La vida no es muy seria en sus cosas," as stated before, was published in *América* in 1945; "Nos han dado la tierra" [They gave us the land] and "Macario" in *Pan* in July and November of 1945. The author has said, however, that the story "Es que somos muy pobres" [Because we are very poor][2] also belongs to this period, a statement that has not been verified:

> What I first published were short stories, in a periodical that we had with [Juan José] Arreola, where we had to pay for our own collaborations. The group is necessary to encourage each other. There I published "Nos han dado la tierra," and then "Es que somos muy pobres." Those were included in *El llano en llamas,* [but not] "La vida no es muy seria en sus cosas." "Macario" belongs also to the first period.[3]

There is a marked difference between "La vida no es muy seria en sus cosas" and the other stories. Rulfo did not include it in *El llano en llamas* [The burning plain] when he collected his stories in 1953.[4] It was not until 1978 that "La vida no es muy seria en sus cosas" appeared, in his book *Antología personal,* together with "A Night's Fragment." The *Pan* stories are entirely different. In them Rulfo demonstrates a mastery of both technique and style in the writing of short stories. They are his first significant works and worthy of a place in *The Burning Plain*. Between

1948 and 1951 he published four more stories in *América,* all collected in his first book.[5]

Since these *Pan* and *América* stories were published before they appeared in book form, they will be discussed first, in the order in which they appear in *El llano en llamas.* The two interpolated stories ("The Man," and "At Daybreak"), not published before 1953, will be analyzed in the next chapter.

"Macario"[6]

"Macario," one of the best of Rulfo's stories, shows a marked improvement over "La vida no es muy seria en sus cosas," not only in technique but also in the treatment of the subject matter, characterization, and style. "Macario" reflects the assuredness of the master storyteller, well versed in the psychology of adolescents, especially those of limited mental capacity. Rulfo expresses in depth the experiences of a young boy—or perhaps a young man; his age is never revealed—whose world is very confined.

The story comes to life and becomes credible because the author had the astuteness to let Macario reveal his own self by means of a long monologue. Through the filter of his limited perspective the reader becomes acquainted with Macario's world. The technique is the same as that used by William Faulkner in *The Sound and the Fury* (1929), wherein Benjy describes his world. Benjy, thirty-three years old and mentally retarded, thinks, "Through the fence, between the curling flower spaces, I could see them hitting."[7] Macario, having been ordered to sit in front of the sewer to stop the frogs from coming out and awakening his *madrina* ("godmother") with their croaking, also thinks, "I am sitting by the sewer waiting for the frogs to come out" (3). Macario and Benjy are narrators interpreting a reality superior to their mental capacities, only partially understood by them. Both Faulkner and Rulfo place their characters in a limited space right at the opening of the stories, and from that perspective the action develops in the minds of the narrators.

For Marcario, the world consists of persons who insist on limiting his activities, especially preventing him from satisfying his insatiable hunger. Macario could very well be the same boy, now grown, whom the gravedigger Claudio was carrying in his arms in the story "A Night's Fragment," who was born hungry and never fed enough. And, like the baby, Macario knows where the food is. He knows that Felipa, his *madrina*'s servant, can feed him from her breast. But if she is not available he can always eat the flowers of the hibiscus, which are as sweet as Felipa's milk. He has also "drunk goat's milk and also the milk of a sow that recently had pigs. But no, it isn't as good as Filipa's milk. Now it's been a long time since she has let me nurse the breasts that she has where we just have ribs, and where there comes out, if you know how to get it, a better milk than the one Godmother gives us for lunch on Sundays" (4–5).

The fact that Macario is mentally retarded and his fear of being punished by the *madrina* if he lets the frogs out give credibility to his monologue, spoken aloud in very simple sentences. This technique is not common in Rulfo, for the monologues of his characters are usually directed to a silent listener. Both techniques are quite effective. Macario's fear of falling asleep and letting the frogs out forces him to talk aloud to himself. Although they never come out, they are uppermost in his mind and serve to relate him to his world. Unconsciously, he identifies his Godmother with the toads. "Frogs are green all over except on the belly. Toads are black. Godmother's eyes are also black." And unconsciously, he expresses his repressed dislike for his *madrina*: "Frogs make good eating. Toads don't. People just don't eat toads. People don't, but I do, and they taste just like frogs" (3).

Macario's world is a primitive one, where people are either good (Felipa) or bad (the Godmother or the boys in the street who whip him). Therefore, the story shares the structure of a fairy tale. The antagonism between Macario and his Godmother, his alliance with Felipa, and the presence of supernatural beings are all characteristics of the fairy tale. However, the hostility between Macario and his Godmother does not give tension to the story, for Macario knows that it is his *madrina* who pays for the food he eats, and he cannot fight her openly. "I love Felipa more than Godmother. But Godmother is the one who takes money out of her purse so Felipa can buy all the food" (3–4). Tension comes from placing two worlds in opposition, the everyday world of sewers, frogs, cats—a world in which people go to church, get hungry, sweep the streets, and do other household chores; and a world populated with devils and suffering souls whose murmurs cannot be heard because the crickets make so much noise. "The day there are no more crickets the world will be filled with the screams of holy souls and we'll all start running scared out of our wits" (7). This technique of placing two worlds in opposition, the *here* and the *there*, would be later perfected and given full expression in Rulfo's novel *Pedro Páramo* (1955). In "Macario," it does not yet predominate. Nevertheless, in this story Rulfo has skillfully created, within a limited space and a limited time, a rich unity of impression which has a powerful impact on the reader.[8]

"Nos han dado la tierra"[9]

In "They Gave Us the Land," one of the first significant stories by Juan Rulfo, the author approaches a sociopolitical subject, the distribution of land by the revolutionary government.

Land reform had been one of the main causes of the Revolution of 1910. Before that time most of the land was in the hands of the *hacendados*, owners who inherited it from their ancestors who, in turn, had received land grants from the Spanish monarchs. It was not until the middle of the nineteenth century, with the Constitution of 1857, that a land-reform program was initiated, but it was not carried out due to the Three Years' War and the Napoleonic invasion. During the Porfirio Díaz regime the villages, which had held land in common since Colonial times, were dispossessed of their holdings, which passed into the hands of *hacendados* or land companies. By 1910 only 5 percent of the heads of rural families held any land, and half the rural population was bound to the *hacendados* by debt slavery.[10] As early as 1906 Ricardo Flores Magón had proposed land reform. Article 36 of his "Plan Liberal" says that the state should give land to those who ask for it. Francisco I. Madero in his "Plan de San Luis" incorporated the idea of land reform but did not have time to put it into effect. In the South, Emiliano Zapata, as early as 1911, took up arms with the cry, *Tierra y Libertad*. Two years later, in northern Mexico, General Lucio Blanco distributed the first land to *campesinos* who requested it. In 1915, President Venustiano Carranza issued a law regarding land reform which formed the basis for Article 27 of the Constitution of 1917, which provides that the necessary means should be taken to divide large landed estates in order to develop new agricultural communities. By 1940, the last year of the Cárdenas presidency, 63 million acres had been distributed. However, after that year land distribution, although it did not stop, declined considerably.[11] The land distributed, however, was not necessarily the best. The old revolutionaries, now in positions of leadership, became the new owners of the most productive areas. The farmers were given land where water was not available. That is the topic of Rulfo's story. It appeared when the government was most interested in industrializing the country at the expense of land reform.

The story "Nos han dado la tierra" tells of a simple incident regarding the delivery of land to the heads of families of a small rural community. The *campesinos* leave their homes at daybreak in order to receive the promised land. Because it is a very hot day, the group begins to dwindle. By eleven o'clock in the morning only a few over twenty men remain, and by four o'clock in the afternoon only the narrator and three others are left. Finally the government representative appears to deliver the land and the deeds. The *campesinos* want the land near the river, but they are given the Llano Grande, which is more like a desert than farm land, since there is no water there for irrigation. It is as hard as *tepetate* ("porous rock"), resembling a dried-up cow's hide which not even a plow can penetrate. The *campesinos* protest, pointing out that there is no water. Ironically, the official tells them that it is *tierra de temporal* ("rainy season farm land"), when he knows very well that it never rains in the *llano*. When the *campesinos* point out that the land is washed out, he tells them that they should not attack the government that is giving them the land, that if they have any complaints, they should put them in writing. They finally give up their attempt to get the land and go to the town by the river, protesting that the Revolution has not helped them after all. Before they had horses and rifles; now they have nothing.

The story begins when there are only four *campesinos* left: Melitón, Faustino, Esteban, and the narrator, whose name is never revealed. These four representatives of the community typify the plight of the *campesinos*. Esteban carries his only possession, a chicken, under his coat. He is a pessimist, as opposed to Melitón, who tries to see the good aspect of the deal. When Melitón says, "'This is the land they've given us,'" the narrator replies, "'What land have they given us, Melitón? There isn't even enough here for the wind to blow up a dust cloud.'" And when Melitón again says. "'It must be good for something—for something, even just for running mares,'" Esteban says, "'What mares?'" (14–15).

The situation of the *campesinos* is made all the more dramatic by the description of the desolate plains, the first description by Rulfo of his native region. He does not identify it geographically, as he will do later, except for the use of the term *Llano Grande*. The oppressive nature of the environment is given emphasis by the use of imagery which, although regional, cuts deeply into the nature of the rural people through its metaphorical associations. The heat of the Llano is so intense that the campesinos even stop talking. "For some time now we haven't felt like talking. Because of the heat. Somewhere else we'd talk with pleasure, but here it's difficult. You talk here and the words get hot in your mouth, with the heat from outside, and they dry up on your tongue until they take your breath away" (12). When a drop of rain falls on the Llano, by mistake, it is "gobbled up by the thirsty earth" (12).

On the Llano there is nothing "except a few scrawny huizache trees and a patch or two of grass with the blades curled up" (13). Even the lizards, "as soon as they feel the roasting sun quickly hide themselves" (13). When the government representative offers the *campesinos* the Llano Grande, they refuse the land; they do not want "this tough, cow's hide they call the Plain," where there is not even "a mouthful of water," where the land is like "a sizzling frying pan," where nothing will take root, where not even the buzzards want to stop. "You see them . . . flying to get away as soon as possible from this hard white earth, where nothing moves and where you walk as if losing ground" (13–14).

The stark nature of the land the government has offered the farmers is contrasted at the end of the story with the land by the river, the land that the *campesinos* want, but are not getting. "As we descend, the land becomes good. . . . After tromping for eleven hours on the hard plain, we're pleased to be wrapped in that thing [dust] that jumps over us and tastes like earth. Above the river, over the green tops of the casuarina trees, fly flocks of green chachalacas. That's something else we like" (16).

The social content in "They Gave Us the Land" is not stated explicitly, as was the custom among the short-story writers of the Revolution. It is casually expressed by the action of the characters and not by any editorializing on the part of the author. Although this social protest against the results of the Revolution is of importance, there is another element revealed in Rulfo's story, and that is the mythical structure of death and resurrection, death being symbolized by the Llano and life by the community by the river. In the Llano there is an absence of living things, of life-giving things like rain, while in the town there is life, the river, the dogs, the people, the smoke coming from the kitchens. The journey of the *campesinos* through the Llano is like a journey through hell, while their arrival at the river and the community is symbolic of their resurrection. The mythical design serves to carry out the social message by giving the story a more abstract structure, which distinguishes it from those of the writers of the Revolution. This combination of two forms of fiction, the realistic and the mythical, places "They Gave Us the Land," and all of Rulfo's fiction in general, on a universal plane.

Rulfo is able to achieve this universality by avoiding, as much as possible, all references to folkloric customs and ways of life of the Mexican people; by eliminating the narrator who speaks more as an ethnologist than as an impartial observer of human behavior, a narrator who presents his personages as if they were subjects for a study on economic problems or social ills, or informants describing their subculture; and finally by abandoning the characteristic style of the narrators of the Revolution, who had inherited the realists' device of reproducing the language of the people without any changes, as if transcribed from a tape. Rulfo's characters are human beings, not social types, and his style is highly literary, quite often poetic.

The two levels of meaning, the sociopolitical and the mythical, are not entirely independent in the story, for the theme of death and resurrection could be symbolically interpreted to mean that there is some hope for the Mexican rural population, abandoned by authorities to a slow death in their communities, without any resources. And the future could be better, could even be as green as the vegetation alongside the life-giving river the four characters in the story first see in the distance and finally reach, even if without land. Rulfo's attitude, here and in others of his stories, is not entirely pessimistic. There is some hope, however dim it may be.[12]

"La cuesta de las comadres"[13]

In the second of the *América* stories included in *The Burning Plain,* "The Hill of the *Comadres,*" Rulfo for the first time makes use of a subject dealing with violence. To tell the story of the Torrico brothers, who are highwaymen, he returns to the technique first used in "A Night's Fragment," the extended monologue wherein the internal dialogue predominates. Telling his story in the present and at an advanced age, the narrator dramatizes the events in the life of the Torrico brothers, his participation in the highway robberies, and finally the brutal killing, by himself, of one of the brothers. With the use of internal dialogue Rulfo is able to abolish time and depict past events as if they were actually happening. The fact that the reader is aware that those acts took place a long time ago creates a distance and therefore ameliorates the impact of their violent nature.

There is a slight difference in the technique used in "La cuesta de las comadres" and "A Night's Fragment." In the latter story it seems Pilar is telling her story to someone in the room where she and Claudio live. After the gravedigger has told her his name and who the baby's parents are, she makes some statements that could only be addressed to a third person, as if she were answering some questions: "He was called Claudio Marcos. No, the baby was not his. It belonged to a *compadre.*"[14] The second part begins with a statement that also could only be addressed to a third party: "He is the same person that is now sitting on the edge of my bed, in silence, with his head between his hands" (151). In "The Hill of the *Comadres,*" on the other hand, there are no explicit statements acknowledging the presence of a listener. The implicit presence of an audience, however, is suggested by some of the remarks made by the narrator;

remarks often repeated, such as "That was the time when everything changed here" (21), "I killed Remigio Torrico" (24), "This happened along about October. I remember there was a real big moon with lots of light" (24); and the final statement which closes the story, "That's what I remember" (28). This technique, which gives Rulfo's stories an epic tone, is related to the structure of the Mexican *corrido*; thus, the stories acquire an authentic national character since the *corrido* is one of the most distinctive Mexican literary forms. It also has a long tradition, going back to the time when the poet and the people came into direct contact by means of oral literature. Epic poems, folktales, ballads, and other popular forms were transmitted from generation to generation by the towns' bards. Rulfo has applied this old tradition to the writing of literary short stories.

In the earlier story, "La vida no es muy seria en sus cosas," the mother talked to her unborn baby. In "La cuesta de las comadres" the unnamed narrator talks to the dead Remigio. Although he knows that Remigio is dead, he talks to him as if he were alive: "He must've been dead when I said to him: 'Look, Remigio, you've got to pardon me, but I didn't kill Odilón [Remigio's brother]. It was the Alcaraces. I was there when he died, but I remember very well that I didn't kill him'" (27). But more to the point: "'Odilón shouldn't have gone to Zapotlán. You know that. . . . You don't know any better than I why he went there to get mixed up with them'" (27). This technique based on communication between the dead and the living was perfected and used to great advantage in Rulfo's novel *Pedro Páramo*. Perhaps "La cuesta de las comadres" is not one of the best stories by Rulfo, but it does point the way to what was to come: stories that take place in his native region, the plains of southern Jalisco, the region Rulfo knows so well; the presence of the common people from the rural areas, not always morally upright; the sustained interior monologue addressed to an implicit audience; the communication of the dead and the living; the revelation of the psychology of the characters by means of actions as seen by themselves; the completely objective presentation of the story; the cool detachment on the part of the author; and the use of a style which, although based on the speech of the *campesinos* of Jalisco, is highly artistic. The placement of fictitious characters in a realistic environment, the arid, wind-swept, eroded land of southern Jalisco, is one of the most distinguishing characteristics of Rulfo's fiction. It began with "La cuesta de las comadres" and has never been abandoned. Rulfo himself has said, "If I located *Pedro Páramo* in Jalisco, it was simply because that's what I know best. I have the unfortunate tendency to place certain imaginary characters in specific geographic surroundings. I like to give the atmosphere of a place."[15]

"Es que somos muy pobres"[16]

In "We're Very Poor" Rulfo dramatizes the terrible consequences that poverty can have upon the lives of a rural family. As he did in "Macario," he lets a boy member of the family relate the story. He tells how a flood might affect the destiny of his twelve-year-old sister, Tacha, and how poverty affected the lives of his other two sisters. Here again, as in "Nos han dado la tierra," Rulfo makes use of a social topic that constitutes one of the most acute problems of mankind, the effect of poverty upon the rural population. What he did was not unlike what Ricardo Pozas A. was doing about the same time in his book *Juan Pérez Jolote* (1952) and what Oscar Lewis did later in his book *Five Families* (1959). Pozas studied the culture of the Chamula Indians and Lewis the culture of poverty by allowing the people to speak for themselves, describing their living conditions in their own words, which not only made for more interesting reading, but also provided a greater objectivity.[17]

The difference between Rulfo and the sociologists is the difference that exists between the artist and the scientist. The sociologist will not change the language of the informants, nor will he organize his material to produce an aesthetic effect. Rulfo, on the other hand, creates his own style, his own characters, his own community; and although they are imagined, they seem to be much more realistic than reality itself. The language of his people, although it springs from popular sources, is highly artistic; the characters are as realistic as those found in Lewis's studies; and the community he imagines is typical of the rural areas of Jalisco, which Rulfo knows so well. But the technique is that of the short-story writer and not the sociologist. The materials are organized to produce a dramatic effect, more than information. The story is presented as a long interior monologue by the young boy who is observing and describing the effects of a flood and speculating on the fate of his sister who is, he says, "here at my side in her pink dress, looking at the river from the ravine, and she can't stop crying. Streams of dirty water run down her face as if the river had gotten inside her. I put my arms around her trying to comfort her, but she doesn't understand" (36).

Tacha does not understand what is happening, that the flooded river has taken her cow, La Serpentina, and that she probably will not be able to marry, for, as her brother thinks, "she has nothing left to count on while she's growing up so as to marry a good man. . . . When she had the cow it was a different story, for somebody would've had the courage to marry her, just to get that fine cow" (34). If Tacha doesn't understand, her father does. He sacrificed to buy the heifer, and now it is gone, and Tacha will follow the way of her sisters into prostitution. "My father says they went bad because we were poor in my house and they were very wild" (34). And the mother, on the other hand, "can't understand why God has punished her so giving her daughters like that, when in her family, from Grandma on down, there have never been bad people" (36).

Losing the cow is the last in a series of misfortunes that the family has endured which began with the father throwing the two older daughters out of the house; the death of Aunt Jacinta; and the loss of the entire rye harvest as a result of the rains. As in other stories by Rulfo, the narrator raises the possibility of a salvation, a hope. The boy speaks of the possibility that Tacha's calf may be alive. "We don't know whether the calf is alive, or if it went down the river with the mother. If it did, may God watch over them both" (33–34). Both, of course, are lost, and the girl will be lost. That is the fate of poor people, whose salvation depends on the life of a cow.

As in "Macario," Rulfo has made use of a narrator of limited capacity. The reader does not know his age, but his reasoning is typical of a boy of imagination who interprets events with a simple psychology. He says, "I still don't understand why La Serpentina got it into her head to cross the river when she knew it wasn't the same river she was used to every day. La Serpentina was never so flighty" (33). He observes the improprieties of his older sisters and predicts, in his naiveté, the future of his younger sister Tacha. He knows that she is growing up and that her parents will not be able to keep her much longer. His last description of her at the end of the story is significant of his understanding of what Tacha's future will be: "The drops of stinking water from the river splash Tacha's wet face, and her two little breasts bounce up and down without stopping, as if suddenly they were beginning to swell, to start now, on the road to ruin" (37). In his mind, the boy associates the swelling of her breasts with the swelling of the river. This is not the only association of Tacha with the river. When she is crying, "A noise comes out of her mouth like the river makes near its banks, which makes her tremble and shake all over, and the whole time the river keeps on rising" (36). When she grows up, Tacha will be gone like her sisters and like the overflow of the river, and her departure will be another step in the family's disintegration, helped by the swelling of the river.

Comparing "We're Very Poor" with an earlier Mexican short story, "Hombres en tempestad" by Jorge Ferretis, both with similar themes and subject matter, the superior art of Rulfo as a writer is immediately apparent. Ferretis's story has a long introduction in which the landscape is described; the characters are introduced by the omniscient narrator; and the message is presented at the end in the form of an essay. The *campesinos* have endangered their lives in the swollen river to save an ox, since the life of an animal is more valuable than that of a man. Rulfo, on the other hand, disappears completely from the story, does not editorialize, does not introduce motifs unrelated to the characters or the anecdote, and does not diffuse the impact of the story with lengthy descriptions of nature or the customs of rural people. There is no question that "Hombres en tempestad" is an effective story, and there are certain stylistic resemblances between the two writers. Nevertheless, when comparing the two stories, it becomes apparent that Rulfo's "We're Very Poor" is more skillfully constructed, and the theme of poverty better expressed.[18]

"Talpa"[19]

In "Talpa" Rulfo takes advantage of the popularity of a religious center in the town of Talpa, Jalisco, to create a powerful story on the theme of love under the shadow of death. Talpa is the town where a Virgin is worshiped for her power to work miracles, especially for curing those who have been declared incurable by medical science. Rulfo, in his story, illustrates the pain, the agony, the misery, and the degradation endured by those who walk for miles to the Virgin with the hope of being cured.

Talpa de Allende, in Mexico, is located in the northwestern part of the state of Jalisco, a desolated region. It was there that in 1644 the image of Our Lady of Talpa became famous. She has been worshiped each year since then by thousands of people from all over Mexico who make a pilgrimage there, especially on 19 September.

Structured as a journey, like "They Gave Us the Land," this poignant story relates the trip on foot from Zenzontla[20] to Talpa by Tanilo, who is suffering from an incurable disease, his wife, Natalia, and his brother. Tanilo had repeatedly asked his wife and brother to take him to Talpa, but they had refused. Finally they decide to do it, for they know that he cannot survive the trip, which lasts a month and a half on foot. Since Natalia and her brother-in-law are in love, they plan to let Tanilo die during the journey. The plan works, but remorse and guilt destroy their love.

The anecdote is given a sense of tragedy by the constant references to Tanilo's deplorable condition, contrasted to the love scenes between his brother and his wife. Here again, Rulfo has skillfully juxtaposed two potent themes, lust for life and the dance of death. While Tanilo is dying, his wife and brother make love. Tanilo's brother, who is the narrator, thinks: "We wanted him to die. It's no exaggeration to say that's what we wanted before we left Zenzontla and each night that we spent on the road to Talpa" (67–68). And yet, each night they made love. "Natalia and I would search out the shadows to hide from the light of the sky, taking shelter in the loneliness of the countryside, away from Tanilo's eyes, and we disappeared into the night. And that loneliness pushed us toward each other, thrusting Natalia's body into my arms, giving her a release" (68). Before dying, Tanilo engages in a dance, a dance of death: "When we least expected it we saw him there among the dancers . . . with a long rattle in his hands, stomping hard on the ground with his bare bruised feet. He seemed to be in a fury, as if he was shaking out all the anger he'd been carrying inside him for such a long time" (72). Soon after that, he dies.

Since the incident is told by Tanilo's brother,[21] it becomes a confession story: "Because what happened is that Natalia and I killed Tanilo Santos between the two of us. We got him to go with us to Talpa so he'd die. And he died. We knew he couldn't stand all that traveling; but just the same, we pushed him along between us, thinking we'd finished him off forever. That's what we did" (66). Tanilo's death, instead of helping the lovers, separates them forever. The journey to Talpa was a happy one for them; the return trip one of self-reproach; the lovers did not even talk to each other. "I know now that Natalia is sorry for what happened. And I am too; but that won't save us from feeling guilty or give us any peace ever again" (67).

Guilt destroys their love. Rulfo opens and closes the story with the theme of remorse. The narrative begins after they have come back, with Natalia throwing herself into her mother's arms, "feeling like she needed consolation" (65), and the story ends where it started, with Natalia crying on her mother's shoulder. Tanilo's shadow will always be between her and her lover, who thinks, "Tanilo's body is too close to us, the way it was stretched out on the rolled *petate* ["straw mat"], filled inside and out with a swarm of blue flies that buzzed like a big snore coming from his mouth" (74).

Tanilo's brother, as narrator, also has the function of registering skepticism regarding the miraculous powers of the Virgin of Talpa. "We were walking along the main road to Talpa among the procession, wanting to be the first to reach the Virgin, before she ran out of miracles" (70). But then, after Tanilo dies, in church in front of the Virgin, during the sermon, he ponders, "Outside you could hear the noise of the dancing, the drums and the hornpipes, the ringing of bells. That's when I got sad. To see so many living things, to see the Virgin there, right in front of us with a smile on her face, and to see Tanilo [who is now dead] on the other hand as if he was in the way. It made me sad" (74).

The story of Tanilo has a great impact because Rulfo structured it as a flashback in the mind of the narrator. Although their journey took ninety days, Tanilo's brother remembers it in a few moments while observing Natalia cry on her mother's shoulder. Rulfo's art can be even better appreciated if "Talpa" is compared to the movie of the same name based on the story. Rulfo himself criticized the film, for the director interpolated scenes not found in the story which destroy its unity and meaning. In an interview with Enrique Vázquez held in 1977 Rulfo said:

There are other films which, they say, are based on works of mine, but in the ones I have seen I do not find anything even resembling them. There is one called *Talpa*. The director wanted to produce a long film, but my story did not fill the time so he enlarged it with things of his own. He placed in the middle of the film a brothel which I do not know what it is doing there; and he also added a couple of extra characters.[22]

Rulfo's story concentrates on the relationship of only three characters without introducing any others, except for the mother, the pilgrims, and the priest, whose presence is essential in its development. Each motif, description of the landscape, and remark of the narrator produces an impact on the reader to give him the impression that he has been there on that agonizing pilgrimage to Talpa, alongside Tanilo and the lovers. With his characteristic economy of expression, his austere style, and his control of emotions, Rulfo has produced one of the most gripping short stories in Mexican literature.

"El llano en llamas"[23]

"The Burning Plain," the story that was selected for the title of the collection Rulfo published in 1953, is based on stories the author heard while in his home town, told "perhaps," Rulfo has said, "by a poor old man at the edge of the fire turning the tortillas: 'You remember when they killed La Perra.'" The voice of the people, Rulfo says, is a voice that speaks to him, "from the deepest of my being and my memory, 'They have killed La Perra, but the puppies remain.'"[24] Recently, Rulfo has also said, "I had an uncle called Celerino. A drunkard. And whenever we went from the town to his home or from his home to the ranch that he had, he told me stories."[25]

As with some short stories of the Revolution, Rulfo's is based on two *corridos* ("ballads") popular in Jalisco and the Central States, "La Perra Valiente" [The brave bitch] and "De Orlachía" [Of Olachea: name of a general], both from the region of Mascota and Ameca (northwestern Jalisco), not far from Talpa.[26] The first of these *corridos* was composed to remember the deeds of a revolutionary soldier known only by his first name, Saturnino, and his nickname, "La Perra." According to the *corrido* "La Perra" died 4 March 1916 at six o'clock in the morning, during a battle between the federal armies of Major Flores and those of Pedro Zamora, leader of a group of followers of Francisco Villa.[27] The other *corrido* also treats of a battle, this one between the forces of General Olachea[28] and Pedro Zamora at Ishaxtla. Of the two ballads the first is the more important for a study of the sources of "El llano en llamas," for there appear the following verses which Rulfo used as an epigraph for the story:

> Decía Catarino Díaz:
> —Nos quieren hacer poquitos,
> Ya mataron a "la Perra,"
> Pero quedan los perritos.

> (Catarino Díaz was saying,
> They want to cut us down,
> They have killed "La Perra,"
> But the puppies are still around.)

Rulfo re-creates through the eyes of "El Pichón" ("The Pigeon") the way in which "La Perra" died, and speaks of his two sons "Los Joseses." However, the story is not about them, but about the Villista leader Petronilo Flores and "El Pichón," the common soldier who is remembering the events. The story opens with a battle between the revolutionaries of Zamora and the federal troops of Flores. "La Perra" is killed and his body is never found. His two sons continue fighting alongside Zamora. The *corrido* of "La Perra valiente" serves Rulfo as a point of departure imaginatively to re-create the life of Zamora, a leader of men, and "El Pichón," a picaresque character who enjoys participating in battle, sacking the small communities, and stealing girls. As the narrator, "El Pichón" relates in a long interior monologue[29] the revolutionary deeds and misdeeds of Zamora's followers during the five years he was with him. The violent nature of the Revolution is vividly portrayed. After he leaves Zamora, "El Pichón" serves three years in prison, not because of his revolutionary activities but because of other crimes. "I got out of jail three years ago. They punished me there for a lot of crimes, but not because I was one of Zamora's men. They didn't know that. They got me for other things, among others for the bad habit I had of carrying off girls" (95). At some unspecified later time he narrates the events that took place. However, the story ends when he comes out of jail and meets his wife, the last girl he had carried off, when she was only fourteen. It is there that for the first time he sees his son and observes, "He was just like me and with something mean in his look," the same observation that was made by Pilar, in the story "A Night's Fragment," about the boy Claudio was carrying in his arms. "El Pichón"'s wife says to him, referring to the boy, "'They call him *El Pichón*, too . . . but he's not a bandit or a killer. He's a good person'" (95). "I hung my head," "El Pichón" remembers, and the story ends.

Some of the content of "El llano en llamas" is very much like that used by the writers of the Revolution, and some of the names, expressions, dialogues, actions, and characterizations are reminiscent of Azuela, but there are elements that make the story a contemporary one.[30] The most important of these is the distance that Rulfo establishes, first between himself and the narrator, "El Pichón," and then between the narrator and the events which he tells about, which took place more than eight years before, since the most recent is the last scene, where he is leaving prison after a three-year sentence. This technique gives the re-created events some perspective and at the same time transforms the historical happenings into pure fiction, the type of fiction that is characteristic of the 1950s, not of the 1930s, when the acts narrated appeared in strict chronological order, related to well-defined periods. "El llano en llamas" partakes of the advances fiction writers had achieved during the forty years that separate Azuela's from Rulfo's stories.[31]

"¡Diles que no me maten!"[32]

"Tell Them Not to Kill Me!" is considered by the author as his best short story. When he was asked the question, "Of all the pieces you have written, which one do you think or feel is best, or you like most?" Rulfo answered: "There is a short story called '¡Diles que no me maten!' That story."[33] And when he selected the compositions to be read by himself for the series of recordings of well-known authors prepared by the National University of Mexico under the title "Voz viva de México" he selected "¡Diles que no me maten!" and "Luvina," another of his favorite stories.[34]

"Tell Them Not to Kill Me!" is probably Rulfo's most dramatic story. The protagonist, a sixty-year-old man named Juvencio Nava, is tied to a log in a corral, where he waits to be executed. He vehemently pleads for his life, and at the same time remembers the chain of incidents that brought him to his present state. Thirty-five years earlier he had killed Don Lupe as the result of a quarrel. Don Lupe had refused to let Juvencio's cattle graze in his pasture. Juvencio had persisted in it, for there was a drought and his animals were dying off. Don Lupe killed one of Juvencio's yearlings, and Juvencio killed Don Lupe. He was pursued by the authorities and had to hide during those years, after having lost everything that he owned. Even at the last moment before he is shot he asks his son Justino, who has come to see after him, but does not want to reveal himself as his son, to plead with the Colonel (Don Lupe's son) for his life. All in vain. He is shot and Justino takes his father's body home.

The attitude of Justino toward his father's death destroys all traces of sentimentality that may have been built up as the result of the sympathy that has been aroused for the old man. Justino refuses to identify himself and plead with the Colonel for his father's life for fear that he too may be executed. He must think of his own wife and children. When he carries the body home on his burro he talks to his dead father: " 'Your daughter-in-law and grandchildren will miss you,' he was saying to him. 'They'll look at your face and won't believe it's you. They'll think the coyote has been eating on you when they see your face full of holes from all those bullets they shot at you' " (107).

The old man never loses hope of being spared from the vengeance of his victim's son. The tragic end, however, is skillfully foreshadowed by the description of the landscape just before the execution. "The early morning hour was dark, starless. The wind blew slowly, whipping the dry earth back and forth, which was filled with that odor like urine that dusty roads have" (103). On the other hand, Juvencio's attitude toward the earth, which he is soon to leave, is one of deep attachment. "There in the earth was his whole life. Sixty years of living on it, of holding it tight in his hands, of tasting it like one tastes the flavor of meat. For a long time he'd been crumbling it with his eyes, savoring each piece as if it were the last one, almost knowing it would be the last" (103). But he still hopes to be saved. "There must be some hope, somewhere there must still be some hope left. Maybe they'd made a mistake. Perhaps they were looking for another Juvencio Nava and not him" (103).

To provide balance in the story, Rulfo introduces a contrast between Juvencio and his son Justino, and the Colonel and his dead father. While Justino is afraid to defend his father's life, the Colonel is determined to avenge his father's death. Juvencio had been hiding for thirty-five years, while the Colonel had been nursing his revenge for the same time. And although he was too young to remember his father, his whole life has been dedicated to search for the murderer. " 'Guadalupe Terreros was my father,' " the prisoner hears him say.[35] " 'When I grew up and looked for him they told me he was dead. It's hard to grow up knowing that the thing we have to hang on to to take roots from is dead. That's what happened to us' " (105). He then remembers the horrible way in which his father died, and adds, " 'I couldn't forgive that man, even though I don't know him. . . . He should never have been born' " (106). This conflict between two deep-seated human drives, the will to live and the desire to avenge the death of a father, provides an emotional impact that does not easily fade away. Through the skillful use of certain rhetorical devices Rulfo creates a very moving story. Dialogue, which predominates and gives the story a dramatic tone; the use of interior monologue; well-integrated descriptions of the landscape; and the alternating expressions of hope and despair on the part of the protagonist; all combine to produce a powerful and tragically dramatic story.[36]

Chapter Four
The Burning Plain:
The Later Stories

Introduction

Some of the fifteen stories collected in 1953 under the title of one of them, *El llano en llamas* [The burning plain], had appeared, as stated in Chapter 3, in the journals *Pan* and *América* between 1945 and 1951. There is no appreciable difference between these stories and the others, either in style or technique. It is not known if some of the latter were written earlier, but not published. It is a possibility but difficult to ascertain, either by internal or external evidence. The problem is not serious, however, since the span of years is not broad, and all fifteen stories must have been retouched before publication in book form.

It is interesting to note that the book opens with the two *Pan* stories, "Macario" and "Nos han dado la tierra." These in turn are followed by two *América* stories ("La cuesta de las comadres" and "Es que somos muy pobres") and two unpublished, "El hombre" and "En la madrugada." The other *América* stories appear next, in the order in which they were published in the periodical: "Talpa," "El llano en llamas," and "¡Diles que no me maten!" Finally, there are six more unpublished stories: "Luvina," "La noche que lo dejaron solo," "Acuérdate," "No oyes ladrar los perros," "Paso del Norte," and "Anacleto Morones." Two new stories were added to the second revised edition of 1970, "El día del derrumbe" and "La herencia de Matilde Arcángel," and one, "Paso del Norte," was eliminated.

It has been observed that the story "The Burning Plain," under which the collection was published, appears precisely in the middle, with seven stories preceding and seven following.[1] From this fact it cannot be deduced, however, that the first seven stories deal with Mexico before the Revolution and the last seven with the postrevolutionary period. That would be too neat an organization. Besides, it could not possibly be determined if the events narrated in the story "Macario" take place before or after the Revolution. And "Nos han dado la tierra," which is placed in the first part, deals with postrevolutionary Mexico. Only symbolically could the stories be interpreted as representing the two Mexicos, those in which the needs of the people are expressed (lack of land, hunger, oppression) and the others showing the failure of the Revolution to solve those problems and tend to the basic needs of the people, the *campesinos*. But even here, some of the stories from the first part ("The Man," "At Daybreak") do not deal with social conditions, but with psychological problems. In them the living conditions of the people are seen only indirectly; they are expressed implicitly, not explicitly. Rulfo himself has stated, although not positively, that the organization of the stories was left to the editors; the story "Macario," he says, "comes first, but it could be at the end; to be sure, the organization [of the book] was left to the editors, I believe."[2]

"El Hombre"[3]

In "The Man" Rulfo has made use of an archetypal structure, that of the hunt, in this case a human hunt.[4] The hunted "man," José Alcancía, has committed a horrible crime. He has killed Urquidi's entire family in order to avenge the killing of his own brother by Urquidi sometime in the past. Alcancía did not want to kill all of them, but it was dark and he did not want to miss Urquidi. Later he repents of his act, " 'I shouldn't have killed all of them; I should've been satisfied with the one I had to kill; but it was dark and the shapes were the same size. . . . I shouldn't have killed all of them. . . . It wasn't worth it putting such a burden on my back. Dead people weigh more than live ones' " (44–45).

The theme of revenge in this story is better motivated than in "¡Diles que no me maten!" Juvencio Nava's crime had been committed thirty-five years earlier, and he felt that he had paid for it many times over, but Alcancía's has just taken place, and the reader can sympathize with Urquidi, who immediately sets out to avenge the crime. The death of Alcancía is not dramatized, but only verified by a third character, a shepherd who had befriended the fugitive and who later found his body, and who is now reporting the discovery to the authorities. The introduction of this third character, essential to bring together the two interior monologues of Alcancía and Urquidi, softens the impact of the killing of the hunted man by the hunter. This establishment of distance is accomplished by avoiding the description of the actual killing (the shepherd didn't see it), and by the humorous account of the shepherd when relating his story to the Señor Licenciado. Although not as dramatic a confrontation as that related in "La cuesta de las comadres," the impact of the killing of Alcancía, which is left to the imagination of the reader, is nevertheless very impressive. The reader can only conjecture as to the reaction of the hunted man when he saw the hunter, whom he thought he had killed. Since the killing of Urquidi's family had already been described, a description of Alcancía's murder would have been an overstatement. There seems to be a narrative pattern in Rulfo's fiction, since the same thing happens in the story "¡Diles que no me maten!" wherein the killing of Don Lupe is described in detail, but not that of Juvencio. The description of their dead bodies is also similar. Juvencio's face was full of holes as if eaten by a coyote, while "the man" was found by the shepherd with "his neck full of holes as if they'd drilled him" (51).

The archetypal structure of the hunt is reinforced by the imagery. The story opens with a description of the man trying to escape from his pursuer. "The man's feet sank into the sand, leaving a formless track, like some animal's hoof" (41). Alcancía, like some animals, had only four toes on one foot. This is a realistic and not a fantastic motif, for it is explained in the course of the story how he had lost his toe. Urquidi, like a true hunter, studies the footprints and assures himself that he is on the right track, since he knows of Alcancía's deformation. "'Flat feet . . . with a toe missing. The big toe on his left foot. There aren't many around like that. So it'll be easy'" (41). The expressions he uses soon after are those of a man hunting an animal: "'I'll go down where he went down, following his tracks until I tire him out'" (42). And even when he thinks about the past, he compares him to a reptile: "'I waited a month for you, awake day and night, knowing you would come crawling, hidden like an evil snake'" (45).

"El hombre," like other stories and novels by Rulfo, contains elements of magical realism, from which it acquires its tone. In brief, magical realism, as opposed to the fantastic, can be defined as a confrontation with reality on the part of the characters. Reality, for them, is magical, and therefore it is necessary to interpret its significance, to go beyond its surface appearance and look for a deeper meaning. However, the world in which these characters move is the empirical world, not an invented world like those found in fantastic literature or science fiction. The characters take their world at face value, never believing that what is happening to them is a dream, an illusion, a vision, or any other subjective phenomena.

They never doubt that what is taking place is actually happening in the objective world.[5]

The night that his family was murdered by Alcancía, Urquidi had gone to bury a baby of his. Later, while hunting the killer, he thinks: " 'I remember. It was on that Sunday when my newborn baby died and we went to bury it. We weren't sad. All I remember is that the sky was gray and the flowers we were carrying were faded and drooping as if they felt the sun's absence' " (44). At that moment, Alcancía was killing his family. Later Urquidi understands the significance of what had happened to the flowers. Blaming himself for having left his family alone, he thinks: " 'The burial of my baby delayed me. Now I understand. Now I understand why the flowers wilted in my hand' " (45). He does not say what it was that he understood, but it is assumed that the withered flowers were trying to tell him that his family was being murdered, and the same can be said of the gray sky.

Other motifs of magical realism are the river, which prevents the murderer from escaping; voices, which do not seem to come from their speakers' mouths; tracks left by the fear and anxiety of the hunted one (" 'fear always leaves marks' "); and finally the description of nature: the path that "climbed without stopping toward the sky" (41); and the river, giving the man a warning that it will swallow him like it "now and then . . . swallows a branch in its whirlpools, sucking it down without any noise of protest" (46).

Another aspect of interest in the story "El hombre" is the narrative technique, which points toward the novel *Pedro Páramo*. In the short story Rulfo experimented with a dual point of view, moving from the mind of one character (the man who is being hunted) to the mind of the other (the hunter), often without any intervention on the part of the narrator to indicate who is speaking. This technique was to be employed extensively in his novel. Also, the story is fragmented, part being told by Alcancía, part by Urquidi, and part by the shepherd. The reader has to put it all together, like the pieces of a jigsaw puzzle. The events are not presented chronologically, but as they come to the mind of each speaker. In general, it can be said that "El hombre" contains certain innovations in content and technique which were to be developed in other stories and finally perfected in the novel.[6]

"En la madrugada"[7]

Rulfo's "At Daybreak" is the story of the death of a farm owner, Don Justo Brambila, at the hands of Esteban, his farmhand, who is now in prison waiting to be tried and trying very hard to remember what actually took place the morning of the accident. The place where the action unfolds has the same name as that where the author himself spent his childhood, San Gabriel; and a farm owner is killed as the result of a struggle over a calf, as in the story "Tell Them Not to Kill Me!" "At Daybreak" opens with a long (long for Rulfo) description of the landscape at dawn, the town in the distance, and the actions of Esteban on his way back to the farm with his ten cows after a night's pasturing. This poetic introduction, in the third person, serves to set the tone of the story. It describes the coming of the new day, the time when the struggle between Esteban and Don Justo will take place. It is the time when nothing is clear yet; it is "at daybreak," and, just like nature, so now is the mind of Esteban, who cannot quite remember what actually took place at that hour. It is the time when the fog lifts, like a curtain, on a drama that is to take place on the stage. "The stars are turning white. The last twinkles go out and the sun bursts forth, making the blades of grass glisten" (56).

When old Esteban reaches the gate of the corral, which has not been opened for him, he is forced to jump over the fence so as to open the gate for the cows. While he is lifting the gate bar he sees Don Justo coming from the loft with the latter's niece, Margarita, in his arms. He hides until Don Justo has crossed the corral to put Margarita back on her own bed, then opens the gate, lets the cows in, and begins to milk them. Becoming angry with a calf, he kicks it. At that moment Don Justo appears and gives Esteban such a beating that he is left, as he says, " 'almost out cold among the rocks' " (57). And that is all he remembers, according to his account to the authorities, for Don Justo was found dead by Margarita and he was accused of the crime.

Through a flashback in third-person narrative the story is retold from the moment Don Justo placed Margarita on her bed. In the next room his crippled sister, Margarita's mother, is sleeping, but awakens just as Don Justo enters, and she asks, " 'Where were you last night, Margarita?' " (59). Justo Brambila leaves the room silently. It is six o'clock in the morning. He finds Esteban mistreating the calf and beats him. Then Don Justo feels himself "blacking out and falling back against the stone paving of the corral. . . . He didn't feel any pain, just a black thing that was dimming his thought until the obscurity became total" (59). Old Esteban gets up when the sun is already high and goes home stumbling and moaning. At eleven o'clock Margarita discovers Don Justo's body.

Ambiguity regarding Don Justo's death is purposely introduced in the story. Although it is most likely that Esteban killed him with a stone, as others say, it is also possible, as Esteban says, that Don Justo died from internal causes. " 'Well, they say I killed him. Maybe so. But he might've died from anger, too. He was very bad-tempered. . . . Everything made him angry' " (60). At the same time, Esteban had reasons for killing him. Inside him, resentment had been building up against his boss. He continues, saying: " 'He didn't even like it that I was skinny. And how could I not be skinny when I hardly eat anything. Why, I spent all the time driving the cows. . . . It was just one eternal pilgrimage' " (60).

There is a great difference in the attitude toward death on the part of Esteban in this story and Juvencio in "Tell Them Not to Kill Me!" Juvencio wanted to live in spite of his age, while Esteban is resigned to die. " 'Memory at my age,' " he says, " 'is tricky; that's why I thank God that I won't lose much now if they finish off all my faculties, for I hardly have any left. And as for my soul, well, I'll commend it to Him, too' " (60). There is another great difference. While Juvencio is highly sensitive to his surroundings, loving the earth and life in all its aspects, Esteban is angry and displaces his internal conflicts by directing them against the animals he tends. Since his whole life has been spent with the cows, he treats them as if they were his equals, as when he wanted to enter the corral, he explained that he " 'didn't say anything to the cows, or explain anything to them; I slipped off so they wouldn't see me or follow me' " (57).

In its structure this story is unlike any other by Rulfo. To develop the anecdote he alternates between an omniscient narrator and another narrator, Esteban, who uses the internal monologue. The characterization is done by means of the external portrait, as well as revelations by the personages themselves. There are subjective transcriptions of the characters' thoughts and feelings, a technique seldom used by Rulfo. After leaving Margarita, Don Justo ponders, " 'If the priest would authorize this I'd marry her; but I'm sure he'll raise an awful fuss if I ask him. He'll say it's incest and will excommunicate us both. Better to leave things in secret.' " The omniscient narrator adds, "That's what he was thinking about when he found old Esteban struggling with the calf" (59).

The story ends with another description of San Gabriel, this time at dusk, as if a curtain were descending upon the stage where the drama had been presented. "Over San Gabriel the fog was coming in again. The sun still was shining on the blue hills. A brownish spot covered the village. Then darkness came" (60). That night the lights are not turned on in San Gabriel. Don Justo owned the lights.

There are certain aspects of "At Daybreak" that foreshadow the novel *Pedro Páramo*. Don Justo is very much like Pedro Páramo, a local *cacique* who becomes angry easily. He is in love with Margarita, a woman he cannot marry, just as Pedro Páramo is in love with Susana, a woman he cannot reach. The motif of incest appears in both works; Margarita is Don Justo's niece, and incestuous relations are suggested between Susana and her father in *Pedro Páramo*. Don Justo is killed by a cowhand, and Páramo by a mule driver. Both killers have grievances against their superiors. When Don Justo and Pedro die, the two towns mourn. "At Daybreak" could very well have been a chapter of the novel; however, it has the structure of a short story, since the important thing is not the fate of the characters (Don Justo and Esteban) as it is in the novel, but the anecdote, a single incident about the killing of his boss by a servant.

"Luvina"[8]

Of the three types of stories mentioned by critics, those of personage, action, and ambience, "Macario" corresponds to the first, "El llano en llamas" to the second, and "Luvina" to the third. The ambience story (*cuento de ambiente*) is a narrative form in which turning point and outcome are not the most important elements (in fact, they could even be omitted); the anecdote is so diluted that it often disappears; but the ambience receives all the attention and becomes the central element of narrative. This does not mean, however, that there is no theme or action, that it is a paralyzed story, a sketch, or a verbal landscape. In "Luvina," there is a central character, a teacher who has lived in Luvina for some years and is now at an inn elsewhere, remembering and relating his experiences to another teacher who is on his way to the same town. The teacher's experiences in Luvina constitute the plot, a well-structured action motivated by the nature of the physical environment of the place, and are told by him in a long dialogue to his silent partner. Luvina, the town where the teacher had taken his wife, Agripina, and his children, had such a powerful influence on him that it changed the course of his life. The story ends when the narrator, who is drinking and finding it difficult to remember, slumps over the table and falls asleep.

There are two types of space in the story, one objective—the inn where the story is being told, and another subjective—Luvina as remembered by the teacher. A contrast is established between the two in order to bring out the stark nature of Luvina, which has become an obsession with the teacher. Luvina is a desolate place, no different from a ghost town, although some people manage to survive there in spite of its deadliness. The stark environment becomes even more fatal by the contrasting description of the place where the story is being told, a place where there is

life, food, children playing, and even a river. In Luvina there is only death.
In the world of the theater it would appear as purgatory, not far from hell.
" 'San Juan Luvina. That name sounded to me like a name in the heavens.
But it's purgatory. A dying place where even the dogs have died off' "
(120). It is located on the top of a hill, covered by the dust of a gray stone
which the constant black wind blows over people and things. When there
is a full moon some people can even see that black wind along the streets
bearing behind it a black blanket. The narrator says that he never saw it,
but he saw something that affected him much more, the ever-present
image of despair. And yet, the few inhabitants dreaded the hour when the
wind died, for " 'When that happens,' " the people say, " 'the sun pours
into Luvina and sucks our blood and the little bit of moisture we have in
our skins' " (120).

In "Luvina" Rulfo creates a magic atmosphere by combining realistic
and fantastic elements and motifs. Luvina is " 'the place where sadness
nests. . . . And you can almost taste and feel it, because it's always over
you, against you, and because it's heavy like a large plaster weighing on the
living flesh of the heart' " (113). The black wind " 'scratches like it had
nails; you hear it morning and night, hour after hour without stopping,
scraping the walls, tearing off strips of earth, digging with its sharp shovel
under the doors, until you feel it boiling inside of you as if it was going to
remove the hinges of your very bones' " (112).

As the story unfolds the reader passes from the real to the unreal, from
the objective world to a phantasmagoric environment. The motifs of the
real world are presented as a counterpoint to the fantastic, unreal world of
Luvina. The description of Luvina anticipates, to a certain extent, that of
Comala in Rulfo's novel *Pedro Páramo,* after the *cacique* has died and the
community has become a ghost town, a dead town.[9]

"La noche que lo dejaron solo"[10]

Among the stories that have the Revolution as a subject are "The
Burning Plain," which treats of the struggle against Victoriano Huerta,
and "The Night They Left Him Alone," about the Cristero Revolt of
1926–1929, the religious war which was the result of the conflict between
church and state during the presidency of Plutarco Elías Calles. In both
stories the heroes are men fighting federal troops, and the action is seen
from their perspective. In the first story the narrator is a common soldier,
"El Pichón," while in the latter the action is presented from the point of
view of an omniscient narrator.

Three *cristeros,* so called because their war cry was *¡Viva Cristo Rey!* ("Long Live Christ the King!"), Feliciano Ruelas, a young boy, and his two uncles, Tanis and Librado, are bringing arms to their men, who are led by "El Catorce." Unable to stay awake any longer, Feliciano falls asleep while his two uncles keep on walking. Feliciano sleeps the rest of the night and part of the next morning. When he finally arrives at the place where they were to meet their fellow *cristeros,* he discovers that the *Federales* have captured and hanged his two uncles and are waiting for him, for they knew there were three. However, Feliciano is able to flee from them.

This simple anecdote is given significance not by the realistic incidents, as was done in "El llano en llamas," or by the tragedy of the two uncles, but by the way in which Feliciano's life is saved. The story opens with Feliciano ahead, urging his uncles to hurry, " 'Why are you going so slow? . . . Don't you have the urge to get there soon?' " (125). In spite of his urgency, he falls behind. Why? Because *el sueño* ("sleep") gets on his back and forces him to stop to rest. "Sleep clouded his thoughts."[11] Sleep gets on his back and forces him to stop walking. This could be interpreted as a natural happening—Feliciano falls asleep in spite of his desire to get the arms to his companions as soon as possible. However, the boy sees sleep "coming toward him, surrounding him, trying to find the place where he was the tiredest, until it was above him, over his back, where his rifles were slung" (125). He slowly falls behind, starts to nod, and "The others passed him by; now they were far ahead, and he followed, nodding his sleepy head" (126). The weight of the rifles and the weight of sleep on his back finally make him stop, and he falls asleep leaning against a tree trunk. He does not awaken until dawn, but believing that it is night falling, he goes back to sleep and does not get up until the noise of some mule drivers wakes him up, with the sun already high.

If Feliciano is saved from the fate of his two uncles it is because, as the narrator suggests, sleep knew what awaited him if he kept going. Nor can it be said that this was a ruse on the part of Feliciano because he feared what was ahead. There is evidence in the story to show that he was a brave boy. One of the soldiers who caught his uncles says, " 'They say the third one is just a boy, but all the same he was the one who laid the ambush for Lieutenant Parra and wiped out his men' " (128). If he remained behind it was because he was overpowered by a force beyond his control.

A possible interpretation of this story is through the concept of magical realism. The boy sees sleep, feels its weight upon his back, and falls asleep against his will. Unlike the story "El hombre," wherein the perspective is that of the characters, the magical occurrences in "La noche que lo dejaron solo" are told by an omniscient narrator in third person, and not directly by Feliciano in an interior monologue. The introduction of this magic motif gives to the anecdote a dimension that separates it from a simple, ordinary story. If not as powerful as "El hombre" or other Rulfo stories, it nevertheless displays his characteristic style, conciseness, organization of material, and thematic expression.[12]

"Acuérdate"[13]

"Remember" is the story of a maladjusted man, Urbano Gómez, as reconstructed by one of his former classmates, the unnamed narrator, who is trying to stimulate the memory of another classmate, who remains silent. The technique is that of the small-town gossip with total recall who knows the life history of every inhabitant and assumes that others also remember it in every detail. The story opens with "Remember" and the speaker uses "Remember," "Try to remember," "Remember that," or "You ought to remember" throughout the story so that his classmate can recall what happened to Urbano Gómez, a former inhabitant of the village. "Remember Urbano Gómez, Don Urbano's son, Dimas's grandson, the one who directed the shepherd's songs and who died reciting the 'cursed angel growls' during the influenza epidemic. That was a long time ago, maybe fifteen years. But you ought to remember him" (133). Often more details are added to help the listener remember. After describing one of Fidencio Gómez's daughters as being quite tall and having blue eyes, a girl whom the townspeople believed was not his, he adds, "and, if you want any further description, she suffered from hiccups" (133). Thus, by adding one insignificant detail to another, the narrator ends by giving a complete picture of the town's life. Like putting together the pieces of a jig-saw puzzle, the reader puts together fragments of the story until he gets the complete picture not only of Urbano's family but also of the whole village. An amusing miniature portrait of one of the inhabitants is that of Urbano's mother:

Remember they called his mother the "Eggplant" because she was always getting into trouble and every time she ended up with a child. They say she had a bit of money, but she used it all up in the burials, because all her children died soon after they were born and she always had masses sung for them, bearing them to the graveyard with music, and a choir of boys who sang "hosannas" and "glories" and that song that goes "Here I send thee, Lord, another little angel." That's how she got to be poor—each funeral cost her a lot because of the [cinnamon-flavored] drinks she served the guests at the wake. Only two of them lived, Urbano and Natalia, who were born poor, and she didn't see them grow up because she died in her last childbirth, when she was getting along in years, close to fifty. (134)

After giving the life history of Urbano's family the narrator turns his attention to Urbano's private life, beginning with his schooldays, when he used to get the best of his schoolmates by selling them everything he could get his hands on. The reasons for his turning bad are not clear to the narrator, who says only, "Maybe he was just that way right from birth" (135). Urbano is expelled from school before the fifth year "because he was found with his cousin Stuck Up down in a dry well playing man and wife behind the lavatories" (135). He is punished at school and at home, and as a result he leaves, only to return years later as a policeman and filled with hate. He kills Nachito, his brother-in-law, after Nachito serenades him with his mandolin. Urbano tries to escape but is arrested. "They say that he himself tied the rope around his neck and even picked out the tree of his choice for them to hang him from" (136). The story ends with the narrator telling his listener that he surely must remember Urbano "because we were classmates at school, and you knew him just like I did" (136).

The conversational tone of the monologue adds credibility to the story. A contrast is established between the narrator, who has total recall, and the person to whom he is talking, who apparently cannot remember Urbano. The many details remembered by the narrator, often irrelevant, amusing, and insignificant, also add credibility. By this technique the author restores the life of the village as it was fifteen years earlier, and reconstructs the nature of the personal relationships existing among the inhabitants. Yet, this is not a simple social document, but a well-constructed short story centered on the character of Urbano Gómez. Although his life is a tragedy, it is told in a light, matter-of-fact style due to the attitude of the narrator toward the events he is remembering. This establishment of distance makes even the death of Urbano humorous, as it is presented in terms that border on the comic rather than on the tragic. The narrator, an expert raconteur, is also characterizing himself, and his personality comes through as clearly as that of Urbano. He is the typical small-town gossip with nothing to do but inquire into the lives of his fellow villagers. Nevertheless, he has a function in the town: remembering its history. He represents the historical consciousness of the village. Without him and his memory the village, like so many small towns everywhere, would not exist. In this character Rulfo has re-created an archetype, the storyteller who is also the small-town recorder of life in the community.[14]

"No oyes ladrar los perros"[15]

Conflict between father and son is common in Rulfo's fiction. "No Dogs Bark" is perhaps one of the most representative stories of this nature. The conflict here is between Ignacio and his father, whose name is not revealed. The structure of the story is made unique by establishing a dialogue between Ignacio, who is wounded, and his father, who is carrying him on his shoulders, at night, to the town of Tonaya. Since Ignacio's legs cover his father's ears, he cannot hear the dogs from the town barking and therefore does not know if they have arrived at the town, of if they are even close to it. He is anxious to hear the dogs, for that means that he can unload his heavy burden and that Ignacio can receive medical treatment. He does not dare put him down on the road for fear that he could never lift him up again. When he finally reaches the town and puts him down, he hears all the dogs barking. "'And you didn't hear them, Ignacio?'" he said. "'You didn't even help me listen'" (143). With these words the story ends. And the reader assumes, as the narrator suggests, that Ignacio is dead.

While carrying Ignacio, his father scolds him for giving his parents so much trouble. Ignacio's last words are, "'Give me water,'" and "'I'm awful thirsty and sleepy'" (142). After that, "His feet began to swing loosely from side to side. And it seemed to the father that Ignacio's head, up there, was shaking as if he were sobbing" (143). When Ignacio asked for water, it reminded his father of the time when his son was born and of his being thirsty all the time. In this way a contrast is established between life and death. "'I remember,'" the father tells him, "'when you were born. You were that way then. You woke up hungry and ate and went back to sleep. Your mother had to give you water, because you'd finished all her milk'" (142).

Not much is revealed about how Ignacio got into trouble. After he is dead, his father feels thick drops, which may be blood, falling on his hair. He thinks Ignacio is crying, and tells him, "'Are you crying, Ignacio? The memory of your mother makes you cry, doesn't it? But you never did anything for her. You always repaid us badly. Somehow your body got filled with evil instead of affection. And now you see? They've wounded it. What happened to your friends? They were all killed. Only they didn't have anybody'" (143). Although he is angry at Ignacio for causing them so much grief, the father still has affection for his son. This is revealed by the alternating use of the familiar *tú* and the formal *usted*.[16] The use of *usted* serves to establish distance. With *usted* displeasure can be expressed.

When Ignacio begs his father to put him down, for he wants to sleep a little, his father tells him, "'Duérmete allí arriba. Al cabo te llevo bien agarrado'" (116) ("'Sleep up there. After all, I've got a good hold on you'" [141]). But immediately after that, the father changes his tone:

—Todo esto que hago, no lo hago por usted. Lo hago por su difunta madre. Porque usted fue su hijo. Por eso lo hago. Ella me reconvendría si yo lo hubiera dejado tirado allí, donde lo encontré, y no lo hubiera recogido para llevarlo a que lo curen, como estoy haciéndolo. Es ella la que me da ánimos, no usted. Comenzando porque a usted no le debo más que puras dificultades, puras mortificaciones, puras vergüenzas. (116)

("I'm not doing all this for you. I'm doing it for your dead mother. Because you were her son. That's why I'm doing it. She would've haunted me if I'd left you lying where I found you and hadn't picked you up and carried you to be cured as I'm doing. She's the one who gives me courage, not you. From the first you've caused me nothing but trouble, humiliation, and shame.") (141)

And then again, "'Mira a ver si ya ves algo. O si oyes algo. Tú que puedes hacerlo desde allá arriba, porque yo me siento sordo'" (117) ("'See if you can't see something now. Or hear something. You'll have to do it from up there because I feel deaf'" [142]). Ignacio, on the other hand, uses only the familiar *tú* when talking to his father.

"No Dogs Bark" reveals Rulfo at his best as a short-story writer. In four pages he presents a drama in which physical and emotional tensions are orchestrated with great skill. By having the narrator recall Ignacio's past life at the moment of his death, Rulfo sets in opposition two climactic moments endured by all human beings. At the same time he touches upon a deep archetypal conflict, that of father and son. By limiting the time, and by placing the events at night, under a full moon, he adds a new dimension to the simple anecdote.[17]

"Paso del Norte"[18]

"Paso del Norte" is the old name of Ciudad Juárez, in the state of Chihuahua, Mexico. The protagonist's experiences after leaving Paso del Norte in trying to cross the river and enter the United States without documents are recounted in a dialogue between father and son after the latter returns to his home in Jalisco. Although his trip is not dramatized in

the story, there is a short scene that takes place in Tlatelolco, a suburb of
Mexico City, where the protagonist works unloading freight cars in order
to save up the two hundred pesos needed for the *coyote* who is to take him
into the United States. However, he never reaches his destination, because, as he was crossing the river with some others, " 'They peppered us
with bullets until they killed all of us . . . while they flashed the lights on
us when we were crossing the river' " (153). His companion, Estanislado,
is killed in the middle of the river and he himself is wounded in the arm.
He is found on the Mexican side by an Immigration officer, given the fare
home, and told never to come back there again.

As do many immigrants to the United States, this man had left his
family in Mexico. He entrusted his father with the care of his wife,
Tránsito, and their five children, but, upon his return, he finds that his
wife has run off with a mule driver and that his father has sold his house in
order to take care of the children. And yet, after all these misfortunes, the
protagonist has not lost faith. Since his father claims that he still owes him
thirty pesos, he promises to get a job and repay him. For the time being,
he is going after his wife.

In "Paso del Norte" Rulfo has combined several themes and motifs
already present in some of his other stories: hunger, poverty, and the
conflict between father and son. But there are new elements: the plight of
the rural people who migrate to the United States to escape the misery in
which they live; the *coyote* system, which exploits them by taking advantage of their ignorance; and the creation of a character who, in the face of
severe adversity, does not lose his faith. Is he, as his father insists, too
stupid to realize that he has been taken in? Or is the story an indictment
against the uncaring attitude of the father toward his son and his son's
family; or against the whole system that forces rural people, however
ambitious and hard-working they may be, to a life of poverty, misery, and
despair, without hope except for the abandonment of country, family, and
friends? These are some of the questions that Rulfo raises in "Paso del
Norte."

Unfortunately, the story was omitted from the second edition of *El llano
en llamas* (1970). When asked why it was not included, Rulfo replied that
it was the editor's decision but that he didn't mind since he considered
"Paso del Norte" to be flawed. "It had two transitions difficult to unite:
the moment when the man goes to look for work as a *bracero* in the United
States and when he returns. There is an internal theme that is not well
elaborated, that is not even worked out. I would liked to have worked on
that story more."[19]

"Anacleto Morones"[20]

In "Anacleto Morones," a story slightly different from the others collected in this first edition of *The Burning Plain,* irony predominates. The story centers upon the questionable character of Anacleto Morones, a religious leader and *curandero* who is either a fake or a holy man, depending upon whose story the reader wants to believe—that of the narrator, who was Anacleto's assistant, or that of the ten church women who want to sanctify him. These women have come all the way from Amula to Lucas Lucatero's home to ask him to testify as to the saintliness of Anacleto, since he knew him well and had married his daughter. Lucas knew Anacleto well enough to believe that he was a fraud and an evil man. His daughter, he tells the women, was even carrying his own child, that being the reason why Anacleto had married her off to Lucas. The women are openly insulted by Lucas and incensed by his blasphemies about Anacleto but insist that he accompany them back to Amula even though they know him to be a liar and a scoundrel. " 'The priest recommended that we bring someone who had known him well and for some time back, before he became famous for his miracles' " (166).

The two perspectives in the story are completely contradictory. According to Lucas, the women want to sanctify a lecherous man. Lucas accuses him of being a religious charlatan and a living devil who " 'left this part of the country without virgins' " (170–71). Before the visit is over, two of the women confess that they had spent the night, although innocently, with Anacleto, and another accuses Lucas of being the father of her stillborn child. Pancha, who had stayed behind after the other women had left, agrees to sleep with Lucas but later tells him, " 'You're a flop, Lucas Lucatero. You aren't the least bit affectionate. Do you know who was really loving? . . . The Holy Child Anacleto. He knew how to make love' " (175). Was Pancha just trying to get even with Lucas, who had insulted her by requesting that she trim off the hairs from her lips before they make love? Or was she really telling the truth?

On the other hand, according to the women, Lucas is a born liar. " 'We don't believe you, Lucas, not for a minute do we believe you. . . . You were always quite a liar and a false witness' " (167). And in response to Lucas's accusation of Anacleto's incestuousness, they say, " 'You've always been one for making up tales' " (170).

However, Lucas does lie to the women when he tells them that he does not know what has happened to Anacleto. The women think that Anacleto is dead. " 'He's in heaven. Among the angels. That's where he is' " (169).

But at the end of the story, in a dialogue that had taken place between Lucas and Anacleto, now reconstructed in the mind of Lucas, the reader learns that there had been an argument between them over the property, and that now the Holy Child is buried in his son-in-law's back yard. "And now Pancha was helping me put the stones over him again without suspecting that underneath lay Anacleto and that I was doing that for fear he would come out of his grave to give me a bad time again. He was so full of tricks. I had no doubt he would find some way to come to life and get out of there" (175).

Through a combination of techniques—question and answer; interior monologue; insinuation; ambiguity; and undocumented statements—Rulfo constructs a fast-moving story and integrates the diverse points of view, each with its own credibility, without revealing the true nature of the events that took place in the past. He skillfully treats the sensitive topics of incest and religious quacks with irony and even humor. There is also the use of a technique not often seen in Rulfo: the holding back of information in order to maintain the interest of the reader. The last question—Who is telling the truth?—is never resolved, nor are the circumstances regarding Anacleto's death.

As the longest of Rulfo's stories, "Anacleto Morones" has the characteristics of a short novelette, such as the introduction of several characters who have well-developed personalities, each one of whom would be worthy of using in another story. In 1960 Miguel Sabido adopted the story to the theater, and it was presented with a degree of success.[21] A motion picture based on "Anacleto Morones" and another Rulfo story, "El día del derrumbe," was produced in 1972 under the title *El rincón de las vírgenes* [The virgins' corner]. Its director, Alberto Isaac, has said that these two stories held a great attraction for him which he could not resist. "'It was a very difficult challenge facing me,'" he says, "'since I had to find the relation between them—in other words, between "El día del derrumbe" and "Anacleto Morones." At first glance they're very different pieces and to find a connecting thread took a lot of work on my part. Certainly the central character of "Anacleto Morones" was played by El Indio Fernández.'"[22] There is no question that there is some relationship between these two stories, especially the humorous aspect, but the differences predominate.[23]

"El día del derrumbe"

"The Day of the Landslide"[24] first appeared in August 1955 in the literary supplement *México en la Cultura* of the newspaper *Novedades* of

Mexico City. It was added to the stories of *El llano en llamas* beginning with the 1970 edition.[25] It is the only story in which Rulfo uses humor to present his subject matter. The one closest to it in this respect is "Anacleto Morones," and it was perhaps this element that led Alberto Isaac to combine them into one single story in his movie *El rincón de las vírgenes.* There is, however, a great difference in the type of humor used in the two stories. In "Anacleto Morones" black humor predominates. Lucas ridicules religion and all it stands for—miracles, church women, saintliness, prayer, and even death. This scorn is directed toward a man who takes advantage of the religious beliefs of the people in order to deceive them for his own benefit. In "El día del derrumbe," the sarcasm centers upon the inflated, insensitive, and often vulgar politician who also deceives the people for his own gain. The characterization in this story borders on caricature. The governor who visits the small town of Tuxcacuexco to survey the damage caused by an earthquake is a politician whose only concern is eating: " 'People were breaking their necks straining them so much to see the governor and talking about the way he'd eaten the turkey and had he sucked on the bones and how fast he was scooping up one tortilla after another and spreading them with guacamole sauce. . . . And him so calm, so serious, wiping his hands on his socks so as not to mess up the napkin he only used to whisk his moustache from time to time' " (224). At speech time he delivers an oration full of meaningless rhetoric: " 'People of Tuxcacuexco . . . I, considering the basis of my ontological and human concept, I say: It fills me with pain! with the pain brought on by the sight of the tree felled in its first efflorescence' " (227). The banquet turns into a free-for-all when the town's drunkard begins to chorus the governor's remarks with the word " 'Exactly.' " When they try to stop him he takes out his pistol and begins to shoot over their heads, and the fight spreads to the street. The cost of the damage done, plus the money spent by the town to feast the governor, exceed the damage done by the earthquake.

The recounting of this simple anecdote is as important as the story itself. In the form of a dialogue between Melitón and an unnamed narrator, who is apparently talking to a group of people, Rulfo is able to create the illusion of reality. The story is unfolded by frequent inquiries on the part of the narrator, who wants to know if Melitón remembers certain details regarding the event. Melitón seems to have a good memory for he remembers the day better than the narrator and even recites the governor's speech, which he had memorized. When asked if he remembers " 'what that guy recited,' " he answers, " 'I remember all right, but I've repeated it so many times it's getting to be a pain in the neck' " (225). The story opens with the narrator's trying to remember when the earthquake took place, " 'This happened in September. Not in September of this year but last year. Or was it the year before last, Melitón?' " (223), and ends when he finally remembers, " 'Now I'm beginning to remember that the roughhouse was around the twenty-first of September; because my wife had our boy Merencio that day, and I got home very late at night, more drunk than sober' " (229).

This story is the only one in which Rulfo uses humor to treat a political theme. Criticism of the government, which had appeared in former Mexican short stories, is not common in his fiction. There is a precedent for "El día del derrumbe" in stories by both Gregorio López y Fuentes and Francisco Rojas González, who used the same device of a politician visiting a small town to see how he can help the people. But Rulfo's story stands out over those of his predecessors because of its incisive humor which he applies to his characterization of the governor to a degree still unsurpassed in contemporary Mexican literature.[26]

"La herencia de Matilde Arcángel"

This story first appeared in March 1955 in the periodical *Cuadernos Médicos* of Mexico City, was added to the collection *El llano en llamas* beginning with the edition of 1970 (145–52), and translated in 1966 by Margaret Shedd under the title "Matilde Arcángel."[27] As in some other stories by Rulfo, the conflict here is between father and son, but with a variation, for the son triumphs over his father. The scene in which the body of the father, Euremio Cedillo, is brought into town by his son is reminiscent of that found in "¡Diles que no me maten!" However, the action here is seen through the perspective of a third party, Tranquilino Barreto, a mule driver who was Euremio's *compadre* and therefore the godfather of Euremio, Jr.[28] He has a set mind and is very opinionated. He says to his audience, for instance, that Corazón de María, their town, is where runts come from, and adds, "I hope that none of you will be offended, but that's my opinion and I stick to it" (188). Tranquilino is narrating an incident to these people which had occurred sometime before. He had been Matilde's sweetheart and was planning on marrying her, but he made the mistake of introducing her to Euremio, who was to be his best man. Soon after that Matilde married Euremio and later had their first child, whom they named after the father. Coming back from the church after the baptism the boy, according to the father's story, gave a hoot like an owl which frightened the horse that the mother and child were riding.

Matilde fell and was killed, but managed to save the child by protecting him with her body. From that time on the father carried a hatred for his son, whom he blamed for the mother's death. Later the son, who has learned to play the flute, joins a band of revolutionaries; and the father, to get even with him, joins the government's troops. The son survives, but the father is killed, presumably by his son, for the boy brings his father's body back to the town. "He rode the animal's haunches, and in his left hand was the flute, which he played with all his might. With his right hand he balanced a corpse slung across the saddle, his father" (193).

Tranquilino, who never stopped loving Matilde, is biased and blames the elder Euremio for her tragic death. "We buried her. That mouth which for me had been impossible to reach was filled with earth. We watched while she sank into the pit of that grave until we couldn't even see the outline of her body. And there, standing like a tree trunk, was Cedillo. I was thinking, 'If only she had been left in peace in Chupaderos she might be alive . . .'" (191). The father is presented as tall and brawny, and the son as weak, "and some people thought this included his mind" (188). His frailty, according to Tranquilino, was not only the result of the accident, but also of the psychological impact of the atmosphere prevailing in his father's home, for "if he looked limp and disjointed . . . it was because he was crushed under a hate as heavy as a millstone. I think his misfortune was to have been born" (188). On the other hand, the father was a "lusty man, so tall it made you mad just to stand next to him and heft the strength of him, if only by looking at him" (188). The father's hatred is so intense that the mere presence of his son seemed to make his blood curdle. In order to deprive his son of his inheritance, he sells his property bit by bit and spends the money on drinking. Yet, ironically, it is the weak son that survives, and the strong father who succumbs.

In "La herencia de Matilde Arcángel," as in most of Rulfo's stories, there is not only the anecdote that is important, but also the act of narrating. The many rhetorical references to this action, on the part of Tranquilino, constitute a story in itself. He begins, as is customary in traditional stories, by stating that what he is going to tell his audience took place sometime before: "Not long ago in Corazón de María there lived a father and a son known as the hermits" (188). After a short digression about how people felt when in the presence of Cedillo, he says, "To return to where we were, I was telling you about those men who lived in Corazón de María" (188). In order that his audience understand the reason for the father's hatred, he must relate the accident that took Matilde's life: "To understand this we have to go back, before the boy was born" (189). Like the traditional storyteller, common among mule drivers who often have to spend the night outdoors around the bonfire, Tranquilino promises his listeners all the details: "I have to tell you who and what Matilde Arcángel was. I won't leave anything out. I'll tell you slowly. After all, we have the whole of life before us" (189). Often the story concerns himself, and he becomes a participant in the story that he is telling his audience. "I'm a muleteer, and it's because I like it, because I like to talk to myself while I'm walking the mountain roads. But the roads wandering in her were longer than all the others of my life and I knew I'd have to follow them because I would never stop loving her" (189). Apparently, some of his listeners are strangers, for he finds it necessary to introduce himself, "Tranquilino Barreto, your humble servant" (190). As do all experienced storytellers, he repeats some of the details for emphasis so that his audience can savor their full significance. The statement, "But what everybody always knew was that he hated his son," which has to do with the story he is telling, is followed by, "I was telling you about that at the beginning," which has to do with the structure of the tale (191). After another digression he goes on with the story, "Well, to get ahead with the thing, one quiet heavy night . . . some rebels rode into Corazón de María" (192). From here on he finishes the story without further interruption. These rhetorical devices have the function of establishing distance between the audience and the event related by the storyteller, used so skillfully by Rulfo here and in most of his short stories.[29]

Chapter Five
Pedro Páramo:
Context and Genesis

Context

With the publication of Juan Rulfo's *Pedro Páramo* in 1955 the Mexican novel reached a high degree of perfection. Critics are unanimous in claiming that this work represents the highest level reached at that point in the development of the genre in Mexico. It is enough to quote the opinion of Carlos Fuentes, today considered Mexico's outstanding novelist. In 1969 he said, "The work of Juan Rulfo is not only the highest expression which the Mexican novel has attained until now: through *Pedro Páramo* we can find the thread that leads us to the new Latin American novel."[1]

The high expression of which Fuentes speaks is the result of a long tradition in the development of the Mexican novel, which has its origins in Colonial New Spain.[2] According to Rulfo, however, the Mexican novel did not attain originality until the period of the Revolution. All novels written before that time belong to Spanish literature. The creation of a national novel, which Ignacio Manuel Altamirano had advocated as early as 1868, when he advised young writers to stop imitating the Europeans and produce a literature "which is absolutely our own," did not take place until Azuela, Guzmán, Muñoz, and others began to write. "The great Mexican novel," Rulfo said, "began with the Revolution. It can be stated that at that time it reached its greatest moment. What came before, like *El Periquillo Sarniento,* belongs to the Spanish picaresque. Even [Manuel] Payno has his place among the Spanish."[3]

Of the novelists of the Revolution, Rulfo has praised Heriberto Frías (a precursor with his novel *Tomóchic*), Mariano Azuela, Rafael F. Muñoz, Gregorio López y Fuentes, Martín Luis Guzmán, and Cipriano Campos Alatorre. In *Tomóchic,* as in the novels of the Revolution, the characters are soldiers, soldaderas, Indians who defend their land, and common people who defend their freedom. The theme is that of injustice; the conflict is between brothers.

Like Frías's novel, the novels of the Revolution and those closely associated with them are neorealistic, a trend that was to appear in Europe only after the Second World War. They contain descriptions of actual events, quite often observed personally by the writers. The characters speak the language of the people, with emphasis on local terms. With these books Mexican literature saw the birth of the contemporary novel, a novel that was to flourish with such works as Agustín Yánez's *Al filo del agua* [At the edge of the storm, 1947], Rulfo's *Pedro Páramo,* and Carlos Fuentes's *La muerte de Artemio Cruz* [The death of Artemio Cruz, 1962].

When the criticism written about the novels of the Revolution is examined, a strange contradiction is uncovered. Unlike Rulfo, most critics consider these novels to be of poor literary quality, more in the nature of historical documents than works of art. Yet, they dedicate long, elaborated studies to them. The novel of the Revolution is that aspect of Mexican literature which has received the most attention, both within and outside Mexico. From the very beginning, critics have reflected this strange anomaly. Representative of Anglo-American criticism is Ernest Moore who, as early as 1941, published the first *Bibliografía de novelistas de la revolución mexicana,* a painstaking work in which more than 260 titles are documented. In the Introduction he observes that more novels have been written about that historical event than any other, a fact that "demonstrates the importance of this literary movement."[4] Yet, in the same Introduction, he states: "Having come *after* the struggle, it was not a theoretical novel, but realistic; more historical and brutal than fantastic and delicate. . . . It was like life itself during those chaotic days, without plot, without composition, without balance, without beauty."[5] But even Mexican critics, among them one who has provided a penetrating analysis of the psychology of the Mexican people, have had little regard for that same novel. In July 1943, two years after Moore's *Bibliografía* appeared, Octavio Paz published in the periodical *Sur* of Buenos Aires a review of the novel *El luto humano* by a Rulfo contemporary, José Revueltas. There he rejected in absolute terms the novel of the Revolution, and realist fiction in general. He says, "The novelists of the Revolution, and among them the great nearsighted talent of Azuela, blinded by the furor of the gunpowder or by the diamonds of the generals, have reduced subject matter to this: many deaths, many crimes, many lies. . . . In this manner they have mutilated novelistic reality, the only one that counts for the novelist. . . .

All the 'Novels of the Revolution' are nothing but reports and chronicles, without excluding those of Mariano Azuela (Larbaud used to say that Azuela reminded him of Tacitus: strange praise for a novelist!)."[6]

As late as 1962 Paz maintained the same attitude toward the novel of the Revolution. In an interview published that year, Claude Couffon asked him this question: "In your judgment, what is the importance of the novelists of the Revolution? I am thinking concretely about Martín Luis Guzmán, Mariano Azuela, and younger, Rafael Felipe Muñoz." Paz answered: "I do not deny the historical importance, so to speak, of those novelists; but, in substance, they do not interest me. Martín Guzmán, Azuela, and Muñoz are naturalistic novelists who described, as witnesses, with great mastery, Mexican society face to face with the Revolution. As documents, their works have capital importance. But for the writers of my generation, for me, they do not open any new perspectives."[7] On the other hand, Paz has nothing but praise for Rulfo's *Pedro Páramo*. In his essay "Landscape and the Novel in Mexico" he expressed the following:

Whereas Malcolm Lowry's theme [in the novel *Under the Volcano*] is the expulsion from Paradise, the theme of Juan Rulfo's novel *Pedro Páramo* is the return to Paradise. Hence the hero is a dead man; it is only after death that we can return to the Eden where we were born. But Rulfo's main character returns to a garden that has burned to a cinder, to a lunar landscape. The theme of return becomes that of an implacable judgment: Pedro Páramo's journey home is a new version of the wanderings of a soul in Purgatory. The title is a (unconscious?) symbol: Pedro, Peter, the founder, the rock, the origin, the father, the guardian, the keeper of the keys of Paradise, has died; Páramo (the Spanish word for wasteland) is his garden of long ago, now a desert plain, thirst and drought, the parched whispers of shadows and an eternal failure of communication. Our Lord's garden: Pedro's wasteland. Juan Rulfo is the only Mexican novelist to have provided us an image—rather than a mere description—of our physical surroundings. Like Lawrence and Lowry, what he has given us is not photographic documentation or an impressionist painting; he has incarnated his intuitions and his personal obsessions in stone, in dust, in desert sand. His vision of this world is really a vision of *another world*.[8]

Paz's opinion about the novel of the Revolution is not an isolated one. Rafael Solana, novelist and critic, had characterized the novelists of the Revolution and also the Contemporáneos who, at the same time, wrote nonrealistic novels, with this sarcastic statement: "But neither Torres Bodet, who fights alone, nor the two thousand novelists of the Revolution . . . 'the Botas stable,' breathe any longer a pure and healthy air. The one

. . . is not preoccupied with filling his pages with truly emotional, human values. . . . The others are unable to deviate an inch away from that 'Rancho Grande' of the novels for which, unfortunately, [its model] came to be *Los de abajo*."[9]

This dislike for the novels of the Revolution or for certain aspects of them among intellectuals and critics, but not among the people who continued reading them, lasted until the middle 1960s. In the *Trayectoria de la novela en México* (1951) Manuel Pedro González, an acknowledged admirer of Azuela and the other novelists of the Revolution, had this to say:

All the so-called novels of the Revolution are fragmentary, episodic, and frequently appear to be reports or chronicles. Each of them focuses on only one aspect or sector, on only one personality or one variant of the terrible hurricane. Not even the three greatest works inspired by the Revolution—*Los de abajo, El águila y la serpiente,* and *Ulises Criollo*—are all-inclusive. In them we only perceive certain aspects or profiles of the Revolution, generally negative and pessimistic.[10]

When that book was published *Pedro Páramo* had not yet been written. However, even though it has some of the characteristics of the novel of the Revolution, González, in a more recent study, praises it, but for other reasons: "Another Mexican novel," he says, "which has also received warm compliments in the whole Continent is *Pedro Páramo,* whose prestige has not declined. This work represents the most accomplished application of the intricate technique used by Faulkner that has been written in Mexico, and it is much superior to the use that José Revueltas in *El luto humano* (1943) and *Los días terrenales* (1949) makes of it. In my opinion, both Rulfo and Revueltas overemphasize technique, and follow too closely Faulkner's methods. This excessive loyalty to the Yankee novelist harms them because it lessens the originality of their works and turns them into a charade that the reader has to decipher."[11]

As late as 1966 John Brushwood, in his book *Mexico in Its Novel,* said that the novels of the Revolution are "lineal accounts, episodic, with sketchily drawn characters. In general, everything—structure, style, characterization, even ideology—is subordinate to each author's need to tell what it was like" (206). If he criticizes the novel of the Revolution because it is loosely structured, he admires *Pedro Páramo* not for its complex structure, but for its thematic expression: "Nowhere in Mexican literature," he says, "has the *caciquismo* theme been treated as well as in

Pedro Páramo. There is not the slightest doubt that Rulfo knows what he is talking about, that he understands his theme, and that he is able to show the reality of it as it had never been shown before. Quite naturally, some readers object to the difficult access to the novel, and some prefer to reject it rather than work for what it says. I can sympathize with the reluctance to participate so actively, but it seems to me that the result is worth the effort" (33).

The above examples are sufficient to show the negative trend that was developing in literary criticism against the novel of the Revolution. However, that began to change in the late 1960s. No better example can be given of the change that took place than to compare the remarks of Carlos Fuentes in 1959 and ten years later. To the question asked of him by Claude Couffon, "How do you explain, after the strong wave of 'the novels of the Revolution,' the silence of the Mexican novelists until the moment of the renaissance of the contemporary novel?" Fuentes gave, in part, the following explanation: "The novel of the Revolution—Mariano Azuela, Martín Luis Guzmán, etc.—was the urgent response to the greatest social convulsion suffered by Mexico since independence. . . . During the dead period of our novel (1935–1950), Mexican literature lived especially in poetry, and the best novelists of today owe a great deal of their language to the work of poets like Octavio Paz, José Gorostiza, Carlos Pellicer, and Alí Chumacero. . . . With the exception of José Revueltas's novels, who is a strong visionary in *El luto humano,* the most perfect image was to be found, during those days, in poetry."[12] In 1969 Fuentes himself pointed out the contributions of the novel of the Revolution not only to Mexican fiction, but also to the new Latin American novel. In his study, *La nueva novela hispanoamericana* (1969), he admits, although begrudgingly, that

the marching people of Azuela, Guzmán, and Muñoz, perhaps in spite of their authors, break with the romantic popular tradition in fiction, with the fatality of nature, which is impenetrable, and the archetypal banana-republic dictator, to expose them as static and transitory realities. *Los de abajo, La sombra del Caudillo,* and *Si me han de matar mañana,* in spite of their possible technical defects, and in spite of their documental ballast, introduce an original note in the Hispanic American novel: they introduce ambiguity. Because in their revolutionary dynamics the heroes can be villains, and the villains can be heroes. (15)

According to Fuentes, the technique of the novelists of the Revolution is put to rest in 1955 by Rulfo with his *Pedro Páramo:*

Nevertheless, there is a compelling lack of perspective in the Mexican novel of the Revolution. The themes at the tip of their fingers about which the authors were itching to write forced them to use a testimonial technique which, to a large extent, did not allow them time to penetrate deeply into their own findings. It was necessary to wait until 1947, when Agustín Yáñez produced the first modern vision of Mexico's immediate past in *Al filo del agua,* and until Juan Rulfo, in *Pedro Páramo* in 1953 [1955], was able to proceed with the mythification of the situations, the characters, and the speech of the Mexican countryside, closing forever, with a golden key, the documental technique of the [novel] of the Revolution. Rulfo converted Azuela's and Guzmán's seeds into a dry and bare tree from which hang somber fruits. (15–16)

One year before Fuentes published his book, Octavio Paz had expressed the same idea about the ambiguity of the novel of the Revolution. To the question, "Where do we see the subversive nature of the Mexican novel?" Paz answered,

The Mexican novel was born with a subversive writer, Mariano Azuela. Although he was not a great writer, at the moment that the Revolution triumphed he denounced it and exposed its secret, shady parts. Another contemporary of Azuela, Martín Luis Guzmán, [created], in his novels, central characters who are old revolutionaries but not heroes. Guzmán does not present to us a world of good and bad characters, in black and white. He is not Manichaean. He reveals the essential ambiguity of man and society.[13]

As recently as 1973 Paz again made reference to the novel of the Revolution. He said to Julián Ríos, "The corruption of the Revolution is one of the thematic constants of Mexican literature. It was born with the novel of Mariano Azuela and Martín Luis Guzmán."[14]

If Paz and Fuentes do not write with enthusiasm about the novel of the Revolution, neither do other contemporary critics. However, there have appeared several very well documented studies, most of them done outside of Mexico. In 1967 Adalbert Dessau published in East Germany his thorough study *Der mexicanische Revolutionroman,* translated into Spanish and published in Mexico City by the Fondo de Cultura Económica in 1972 under the title *La novela de la Revolución mexicana.* In England, in 1971, John Rutherford published his study *Mexican Society during the Revolution,* and in 1972 his *Annotated Bibliography of the Novels of the Mexican Revolution of 1910–1917.* More recently Marta Portal has published a thorough study of the novel under the title *Proceso narrativo de la Revolución mexicana.*[15] She goes beyond the study of the period, including Yáñez, Rulfo, Fuentes, Elena Garro, and other younger novelists that have written about the Revolution, such as Jorge Ibargüengoitia, Fernando del Paso, and Elena Poniatowska.

It must be kept in mind that during that "dead period of our novel" there were other works being written, sometimes by the same authors, which utilized innovative techniques unlike those which critics attribute to the novel of the Revolution. Much more significant than *The Underdogs* from the point of view of its form is the short novel *La Malhora,* which Azuela published in 1923. Here he introduced into Mexican fiction techniques that foreshadow such novels as *Al filo del agua* and even Fuentes's *La región más transparente* (1958). In *La Malhora* Azuela makes use of a dislocated structure (characterized by the overlapping of the time element), the fragmentary scene, the flashback, the distorted plot, and the unfinished characterization. The most striking change in technique is the use of unrelated juxtaposed scenes. This spatial arrangement makes this novel one of the precursors of Rulfo's *Pedro Páramo.*

In 1943 Revueltas published *El luto humano* (translated into English under the title *The Stone Knife*), a novel which in some respects shows the influence of Azuela, Guzmán, and López y Fuentes, but in which that of Faulkner predominates. Rulfo has denied that either he or Revueltas was influenced by Faulkner.[16]

The following year, 1944, Rubén Salazar Mallén published a novelette, *Soledad* [Loneliness], in which he carries the psychological process further than Revueltas had done. In *El luto humano* we still find social preaching, but in *Soledad* nothing remains but the interest in the psychological presentation of the central character, Aquiles Alcázar, a government worker in Mexico City haunted by a persecution complex. In order to present the psychological aspect of Alcázar's life, the author makes use of the stream-of-consciousness technique, which was later to be amply utilized by both Yáñez and Rulfo.

Some critics may point out that these novels lack depth and complexity. This certainly could not be said of *Al filo del agua* (1947) by Agustín Yáñez, a novel that takes place in a small town in Jalisco, as does *Pedro Páramo.* Some critics consider this novel, *At the Edge of the Storm,* a novel of the Revolution, since it explains better than history books the causes of the Revolution. The difference between this novel and *Pedro Páramo* is to be found in the style: Yáñez is dense, almost baroque, while Rulfo stylizes the speech of the *campesinos,* and poetic prose predominates. Rulfo himself has written a review of a later Yáñez novel, *La tierra pródiga* [The prodigal land, 1960], which he has called "one of the great works of fiction in Mexican literature."[17]

On 21 August 1965 Rulfo delivered a lecture on the contemporary novel at the Institute of Arts and Sciences of Chiapas. He opened by excusing himself for not speaking about the Mexican novel. However, he stated that he was well acquainted with the authentic values in Mexican fiction, and mentioned Rosario Castellanos, Agustín Yáñez, José Revueltas, and Eraclio Zepeda. Then he went on to discuss the contemporary novel in the United States and Europe.[18] In several interviews, however, he has passed judgment on Mexican fiction. Of the novelists of the Revolution he has expressed admiration for Rafael F. Muñoz, whose novel *Se llevaron el cañón para Bachimba* [They took the cannon to Bachimba, 1941] has great merit because "the central hero, Pascual Orozco, knows perfectly well that he is going down to defeat, while his followers do not know why they are fighting."[19] Of Gregorio López y Fuentes he admires the novel *Campamento* (1931), which he has called "a complete, well-rounded work."[20] He has also praised the novels of Guzmán, Azuela, Mauricio Magdaleno, and Cipriano Campos Alatorre. Of the authors who have published since 1955, he has high regard for Salvador Elizondo, Carlos Fuentes, Rosario Castellanos, Juan José Arreola, Elena Garro, Vicente Leñero, and Fernando del Paso.[21]

Part of the action of Rulfo's novel *Pedro Páramo* takes place during the days of the Revolution, but unlike the short story "El llano en llamas," the novel does not make use of the technique of the fiction of the Revolution. As several critics have pointed out, with *Pedro Páramo* the novel of the Revolution comes to an end, and a new trend is established. It is for this reason that the novel is of importance in the development of Mexican fiction. As a work of art, it marks a high artistic achievement.

The armed aspect of the Revolution ended two years before Rulfo was born, but during the presidencies of Obregón and Calles (1920–1928) the country was still in a state of turmoil, especially during the period of the Cristero Revolt. As a child and youth, Rulfo had the opportunity to hear stories about the Revolution and to experience at first hand the religious war. He himself has said that he "experienced the Cristero war, first in my hometown and then in Guadalajara, between 1926 and 1928. I was in my town during the first skirmishes. I was about eight when the priest of San Gabriel left his library for safekeeping in my grandmother's home, before they expropriated the parish and turned it into a barracks."[22] Those early experiences color all his fiction.

Genesis

The genesis of *Pedro Páramo* really begins with the writing of the short stories, ten years before the novel appeared. Rulfo has said that he began to think about the novel that early. *"Pedro Páramo,"* he said to an interviewer, "came from an earlier period. It was, it can be said, almost planned about ten years before. I had not written a single line when it was already turning in my mind."[23] The setting, the characters, the tone, and the narrative devices found in the stories reappear in the novel. The great difference is that in the novel all the people are dead. Why he selected the rural Mexico of his boyhood and not an urban setting was perhaps due to his dissatisfaction with city life, and also because he had been unable to give expression to that kind of life in "El hijo del desaliento," his first attempt at writing a novel. "The city," he said, "seemed intolerable to me. I did not belong to that world, I was strange to it. Then I began to think about the previous period, that of my childhood and youth. It appeared to me to be a golden age. I felt it to be so close to me that I found it difficult to detach myself from it."[24]

Although Rulfo had thought about the plot of the novel ten years before the work was published, the idea of its structure did not come to him until later, when he visited the town where he had spent his early years and where, instead of finding a paradise, he found a ghost town. Speaking of this, he said:

Although the idea was with me, I had not written a single page. And then something happened that gave me the key to unravel that thread that was still woolly. It was my going back to the town where I had lived 30 years earlier, and I found it abandoned. It is a town I had known, of about seven to eight thousand inhabitants. When I arrived there were only 150 persons there. . . . The doors were locked up. The people had left.[25]

During a conversation which I had with Rulfo in Guadalajara in 1962 I asked him, "What stimulus led you to write *Pedro Páramo?"* *"Pedro Páramo,"* he answered, "is the result of a desire to bring a dead town back to life. The dead town lives again in the imagination of the person-ages. . . . I also lived in San Gabriel, a small but prosperous town. When I returned years later, the community was decimated. That caused a great impression on me. I discovered that the decadence of the town had been the result of the local *cacique's* actions."[26]

San Gabriel appears with its own name in the story "En la madrugada," as Luvina in the story of the same name, and finally as Comala in *Pedro*

Páramo. In an earlier version of the first chapter of the novel, however, the town was not called Comala but Tuxcacuexco, which is a real town not far from San Gabriel.[27] The change to Comala was most appropriate, since the word helps to create the image of the furnacelike atmosphere that prevails in the town. The name change was deliberate, as Rulfo explained: "The name does not exist, no. The town of Comala is a progressive, fertile town. But the derivation of comal—a comal is an earthenware utensil that is placed over the embers for the purpose of heating the tortillas—, and the heat that prevails in that town was what gave me the idea of the name. Comala: the place over the embers."[28]

The locale of the novel and the stories "En la madrugada" and "Luvina" is San Gabriel, but it could be any town in the region where Rulfo was born, for they all have the same features. They are all located in a region which Rulfo has described as depopulated, the people having gone either to the Pacific Coast, the high plains, or the United States.[29]

As Ricardo Estrada has pointed out, the story "Luvina" can be considered "the strongest evidence available regarding the gestation of the ambience of *Pedro Páramo,* and perhaps it could be stated that it contains the germ from which the novel grew."[30] That Comala and Luvina are one and the same place to Rulfo can be seen from his description of San Gabriel which inspired him to write the novel. "I had the opportunity to be there one night, and it is a town where the wind blows constantly; it is at the foot of the Sierra Madre. And at night the casuarinas bellow and howl. And the wind. Then I understood that loneliness of Comala, of that place."[31] Most critics have observed the similarity between the two towns. Rodríguez Alcalá compares them: "If Comala is a town of dead people, of ghosts, Luvina is a town of living dead. . . . If in Comala there are only ghosts, the men and women of Luvina seem like ghosts."[32]

In "En la madrugada," the reference to San Gabriel is explicit. The action takes place on the outskirts of the town; however, the description of the ambience, as opposed to that in "Luvina," is subordinated to the storytelling and the anecdote. Nor is it suggested that the environment motivates violence in the characters, as is done in other stories and in the novel. Of this, Rulfo has said that "the heat, the sultry weather, and the misery that those people suffer, well, I believe they are the cause of their violent character."[33]

The Cults of Violence and Death

It has been said of Rulfo that he is "the greatest single exponent of the cult of death in Mexican literature."[34] He has probably gained this unusual reputation because of his preoccupation with death which is perhaps the element that more than any other pervades his fiction. It is rooted in his personal experiences, and the same can be said of violence. "To be sure," Rulfo has said, "almost all the country's tropical areas are violent. . . . There are reasons for that. In the first place they are isolated regions. The tropics give the inhabitants a very special characteristic, where life matters little."[35]

This preoccupation with the theme of death in Rulfo extends to the town, the region, and even the animals and vegetation. Towns in his native region are dead because the environment is dead. The few people who remain there are prevented from leaving because of their dead ancestors. "Their ancestors," according to Rulfo, "tie them to the place. They don't want to leave their dead." If they move, "they carry their dead on their shoulders."[36]

The presence of death predominates in most of Rulfo's stories, and it is usually violent, as in "The Hill of the *Comadres*," where there are several killings. The phrase "I killed . . ." is repeated throughout the stories. In "Talpa" the death of Tanilo becomes a dance of death; in "El llano en llamas" death becomes an amusement; in "Remember" the man who is to be hanged puts the noose on his own neck; in "No dogs bark" Ignacio dies in the arms of his father, but as the result of a violent fight; in "Paso del Norte" those who try to cross the river are killed like dogs; in "Anacleto Morones" the dead have to be contained to prevent their coming back to take revenge; and in "La herencia de Matilde Arcángel" her death and that of her husband are violent. In "The Man," "At Daybreak," and "The Night They Left Him Alone," there are also violent deaths. And all of them become sacrificial victims in a rite that has been repeating itself since pre-Hispanic times. "Death," René Girard has observed, "is the ultimate violence that can be inflicted on a living being. It is therefore the extreme of maleficence. With death a contagious sort of violence is let loose on the community."[37]

The short stories of Rulfo serve as a prelude for the novel *Pedro Páramo*, which is an orchestration of the theme of death. It begins with the arrival of Juan Preciado at the dead town of Comala, and ends with the death of Pedro Páramo, who is killed by his son Abundio. In the town the dead talk about killings and death, and in their graves they continue their conversations about death.

This preoccupation with death and violence is doubtless the result of the many encounters that Rulfo had with death—the Revolution, the Cristero Revolt, and especially the violent deaths of his relatives. His father, he told an interviewer, was killed while running away; his uncle was assassinated;

his grandfather was strung up by the thumbs and lost them. "They all," he says, "died at an early age, at the age of 33," for where they lived "was, has been until recently, a violent zone."[38] However, at a lecture given at Stanford University the night of November 4, 1982, Rulfo stated that he does not want to talk or write about death any more.

Chapter Six

Pedro Páramo: Structure and Imagery

Souls in Purgatory

Pedro Páramo, Rulfo has said, is the story of a dead town inhabited by dead people. My question, "How did you come upon the idea of creating characters already dead?" was answered by Rulfo with these words:

Here in the towns of Mexico the idea persists that the souls doing penance visit the living. Even today, on the roads wherever there is a grave people throw a stone on top of it, which means that they have said a Pater Noster for the salvation of the dead person's soul. In the novel, they are all dead. When Juan Preciado arrives in town with the muleteer he is already dead. Then, the town comes to life once more. That has been my purpose, to give life to a dead town.[1]

Pedro Páramo, of course, is not the first novel in which dead persons appear. As a rule, however, there are also living characters and they may or may not interact with the dead. Usually the dead world is seen from the perspective of the living, as in Dante's *Purgatorio,* where the souls are very much surprised to see a living person, whom they recognize because of his breathing:

> L'anime che si fur di me accorte,
> per lo spirare, ch'io era ancor vivo,
> maravigliando diventaro smorte. (II: 67–69)

> (The souls who had observed me
> by my breathing that I was yet alive,
> marveling grew pale).

In Rulfo's purgatory, however, the problem of the interaction between the dead and the living does not occur, since all are dead, although they act as

75

if they were alive. Rulfo is not concerned with establishing a transition from life to death. Furthermore, the reader is not told that the personages are dead. Since this purgatory is located on this earth and not in an imaginary space, he must deduce that fact himself, and critics have debated as to who is dead and who is alive. When Juan Preciado arrives at Comala he finds a dead town; but he himself is already dead and is only remembering his arrival sometime later, in the grave.

Comala is a town of ghosts, souls in penance, echoes, and disembodied voices. Donis's sister exclaims, "'The nights are sheer terror. If you could just see all the souls that walk loose in the streets. . . . As soon as it gets dark they start coming out, and we're all afraid of seeing them. There's so many of them, and so few of us, we don't even try to pray for them so their souls can rest. Our prayers aren't enough for all of them.'"[2]

Because of the many souls begging for prayers, Comala is full of murmurs. In fact, the novel was to be called "The Murmurs," and one of its chapters was published before 1955 with that title.[3] The action takes place in that purgatory which is Comala, and the characters are all dead souls. The plot deals with the activities of Pedro Páramo, the local *cacique* ("boss") who accumulated wealth by robbery and assassination but who, in the end, allows himself to be killed by one of his sons after having failed in the fulfillment of his greatest desire, to possess the love of Susana San Juan. With his death Comala dies, until Rulfo resurrects it as if with a magic wand.

Although the novel is the story of Pedro Páramo, Rulfo has said that he is not the central figure but that Comala, the village, is the protagonist. To the question posed by Joseph Sommers, "How do you interpret the fact that some critics say that *Pedro Páramo* is an obscure novel?" Rulfo gave the following answer, "Well, for me also, to be sure, it is obscure. I don't think it is a novel easy to read. Above all I tried to suggest certain aspects [of the plot], not express them. I wanted to close the chapters in a total manner. It is a novel where the central personage is the village. You must notice that some critics take Pedro Páramo to be the central character. But it is the village."[4] There is no question as to the importance of the atmosphere in the village and its dead inhabitants, but above them the figure of Pedro Páramo stands out. The whole town depends for its survival on his whims. His life gains in importance as it is reconstructed from three different points of view as seen by his son Juan Preciado, as seen by the inhabitants of Comala, and as seen by the omniscient narrator. His characterization is thus given depth and complexity. By putting together the three versions, the reader becomes better acquainted with Pedro

Páramo than with any other character, with the possible exception of Susana San Juan, since she affected Pedro's entire life, and her death was the cause of the death of the town.

Pedro Páramo rose from poverty to become the most dominant figure in Comala. Through premeditated steps he gains in power and wealth and acquires most of the land surrounding the town. First he marries Dolores Preciado, whom he does not love, in order to take possession of her inherited land properties. He later abandons her and their son Juan. He obtains the land of Aldrete, who had refused to sell it to him, by having Aldrete assassinated. Finally, with the help of his overseer Fulgor and others, he becomes the most powerful man in Comala, feared and hated by all. His favorite son, Miguel, lives violently, raping and killing without fear, as he knows that his father controls the authorities. Páramo, just as lawless and violent, is nevertheless frustrated by his inability to gain the love of Susana San Juan, his boyhood sweetheart. Susana marries Florencio, who drowns soon afterward, and she returns home to live with her father. In order to marry her despite her father's objections, Pedro Páramo has her father assassinated. However, it is too late for happiness, as Susana is now insane. When she dies Comala's church bells ring for three days. The people of the neighboring villages, thinking that there is a fiesta, come to celebrate. In anger, Pedro decides to let the town die. He sits down in his favorite chair and stays there until his illegitimate son Abundio comes to plead for help. Pedro refuses to listen to him and Abundio, who is intoxicated, kills him. The novel ends with the following description of Pedro Páramo's death, "He leaned against Damiana and tried to walk. After a few steps he fell down, pleading within but not speaking a single word. He struck a feeble blow [*un golpe seco*] against the ground and then crumbled to pieces as if he were a heap of stones" (123).

Pedro Páramo is representative of the *cacique* common in Mexico's rural areas, and especially in the tropical regions. Rulfo has given him a place alongside other famous literary archetypes. Although there are many Mexican novels in which the *cacique* is the protagonist or has an important part, Pedro Páramo is his best representative, for he is not only a *cacique* in the political sense, but also a king in the mythical sense.[5] As to the origin of Pedro Páramo, Rulfo has said:

I do not know from where the personage Pedro Páramo came. I never met a person like that. I do not consider it easy to classify him. I believe he is a *cacique*. *Caciques* are plentiful in Mexico. But their attitudes, their acts, are medals with which the people decorate them. I mean, I do not know if there ever was a *cacique* who made his own revolution to defend himself from the Revolution. But he can be classified by other means: he is, for example, never generous; on the contrary, he is an evildoer. He forms, with others, part of a consciousness, a way of thinking, a mentality that most likely does exist.[6]

As a *cacique,* Pedro Páramo imposes his authority by the fear inspired by his violence. When a boy, someone had killed his father, Lucas Páramo, at a dance. After he attains power he decides to avenge that death. He does not know who killed his father; only the town where the killer lives. To be sure that his revenge does not fail, he kills all the .men of the town, indiscriminately. Besides his cruelty, Pedro Páramo is also characterized by his hatred. When Juan Preciado asks Abundio, "'Do you know Pedro Páramo? . . . Who is he?'" Abundio answers, "'He's hate. He's just pure hate'" (4).

Years after Pedro's death, Juan Preciado arrives in Comala searching for him, as instructed by his mother, Dolores. With his arrival, seven days after his mother's death, the novel opens: "I came to Comala because I was told that my father, a certain Pedro Páramo, was living here. My mother told me so, and I promised her I would come to see him as soon as she died" (1). He is expecting to find a town surrounded by well-cultivated, green fields, inhabited by happy people, according to what his mother had told him. Instead, he finds a ghost town, located in an arid region, without human, animal, or vegetable life, a town populated by souls doing penance whose voices, murmurs, and whispers fill the air and drive him to his death two days later. He was in search of a Paradise, and instead found a Purgatory.

Through these voices, these echoes of voices heard by Juan Preciado, the town of Comala comes to life once more. The other world becomes this world as if by a magic spell. Life and death are one and the same. The personages have the characteristics of the dead but also of the living. When someone dies, he continues to execute his daily activities. Miguel Páramo is killed as he fell from his horse one night while returning home from a visit to one of his many mistresses. Yet he continues to visit his friend and to behave as he did before he died. Time has been suspended. The line between life and death has been erased. By means of this literary device Rulfo is able to structure the plot by juxtaposing often unrelated narrative fragments without having to fall back on the chronological and spatial sequences to which the reader is accustomed. The action can change from the present to the past and back again to the present, and in space from one location to another without the need of introducing formal rhetorical transitions. And yet, there is order in this apparent disorder.

The most important narrative sequences, all related (but subordinated) to that of Pedro Páramo, are those of his two wives, Susana and Dolores, and those of his sons Miguel Páramo, Juan Preciado, and Abundio Martínez. Other narratives, to which less attention is given but which are no less important in the novel as a whole, are those of Fulgor Sedano, Father Rentería, Dorotea "La Cuarraca," Damiana Cisneros, and Donis and his sister. These and other less important personages (Eduviges, Florencio, El Tilcuate, and Gerardo Trujillo) are all, in some way or other, related and dependent upon Pedro Páramo, and often abused by him. Of all these characters, only six have direct communication with Juan Preciado, the central narrator, who often delegates the narration to them; they are Abundio, Eduviges, Damiana, Dorotea, Donis, and Donis's sister. He is informed about the others by Dorotea from her grave and by voices he first hears in Comala and then from neighboring graves, especially that of Susana.

Susana, daughter of the miner Bartolomé San Juan, first appears, as seen by Pedro Páramo, as an idealized woman, who motivates his actions throughout his life. "'Do you know, Fulgor,'" Pedro says to his overseer, "'she's the most beautiful woman in the world'" (83). But, like Dante, he is unable to reach his Beatrice. And Susana, unlike Beatrice, has a tragic life. Because of her father's greed, she was forced as a girl to descend into a cave in search of gold but where only a crumbling skeleton was to be found. The only happy days of her life are those she spent with her first husband, Florencio, who unfortunately died early. She then goes back to live with her father, who abuses her. By the time she marries Pedro she has lost her mind. Nevertheless, she continues to influence him, even beyond death.

According to what Rulfo has said, Susana is the protagonist of the novel:

Susana San Juan was always the central personage. Susana San Juan was an ideal thing, a woman idealized to such a degree, that I could not find out who idealized her. Then I imagined, or learned, that Susana San Juan was buried in that town.[7]

Susana's origin, like that of Pedro Páramo, is not clear in Rulfo's mind. "I do not know either where Susana San Juan came from. Perhaps she is a sweetheart I once imagined I had. And I constructed *Pedro Páramo* around her and around the town."[8]

Among the minor characters, Dorotea "La Cuarraca" is worthy of attention, for she has both structural and thematic functions throughout the novel. First she helps to bury Juan Preciado, and then she sits to wait for death to take her. She is buried in the same grave with Juan, and the dialogues they sustain serve to reveal the history of Comala and their inhabitants. Dorotea's death, as described by herself, is told in terms of Christian beliefs:

"And your soul? Where do you think it's gone?"
"It must be wandering around up there on earth, like all those others, looking for people to pray for it. . . . When I sat down to die, it told me to get up again and keep on living, as if it still hoped for some miracle that would clean away my sins. But I wouldn't. 'This is the end,' I told it. 'I can't go any farther.' I opened my mouth so it could leave, and it left. I felt something fall into my hands. It was the little thread of blood that had tied it to my heart." (64)

On the other hand, Dorotea also symbolizes La Llorona, the mythical pre-Hispanic woman in search of her lost children. She walks about carrying a bundle believing it is her baby. In one of her dreams the two myths unite in a syncretic image:

"I carried him with me everywhere I went, wrapped up in my rebozo, and suddenly I lost him. . . . I arrived in Heaven and looked all over to see if I could recognize my son's face among the angels. It wasn't any use. Their faces were all the same, every one of them." (58–59)

Finally, from Heaven they send her back to earth, and tell her to rest a little longer, "'and try to be good so you won't stay so long in Purgatory'" (59). And in Purgatory she stays, for her sins cannot be easily forgiven, especially her activities as procurer of girls for Miguelito Páramo.

Structure

The aspect of *Pedro Páramo* that has elicited the greatest controversy has been its structure. The first critics, Alí Chumacero, James Irby, and José Rojas Garcidueñas, expressed dissatisfaction with the novel, for they saw it as an example of the disintegration of narrative form. For Chumacero, the novel lacks a center, a core around which the several narrative levels can be integrated. "The principal flaw of the novel," he wrote, "is to be found in the plan utilized to write it. . . . Without a nucleus, without a central point around which the action can be integrated, its reading leaves us at the end with a series of scenes put together only by the isolated value of each one. Let us not forget, however, that this is the first novel of our young writer."[9]

Doubtless influenced by Chumacero's review, Irby considers the novel as a collection of stories ("novela cuentística," he calls it), and expresses the opinion that the order of the scenes could be altered "without producing any appreciable change in the total effect of the work."[10] Another critic influenced by Chumacero's review was José Rojas Garciadueñas, whose reaction was perhaps the most negative. He felt *Pedro Páramo*'s structure had been "deliberately turned upside down and mixed up. . . . What is new is that Rulfo took the three narrative lines, a, b, and c, cut them in fragments, shuffled them, and placed them back together again at random, without a plan or design to organize the whole."[11] A more recent critic, John Brushwood, although accepting the structure of the novel, expresses some reservation as to the advisability of using several points of view. "The narrative viewpoint," he wrote, "is varied and changes as is required by Rulfo's reconstruction of reality. It is possible that the author is subject to criticism on this last point. It may be that the frequent changes make the novel unnecessarily difficult, but I am inclined, after several readings, to believe that the author is right."[12]

In the same year that *Pedro Páramo* appeared, Carlos Blanco Aguinaga published the first study of the novel. In this study the point of departure is that the work is a coherent and well-structured artifact. The novel, he said, "has a very strict structure, where there is no apparent separation of the parts, which would break the unity of that moment of time, which is the whole narration."[13] His analysis of the structure of *Pedro Páramo* has been elaborated upon by other critics, among them Mariana Frenk, Luis Leal, Hugo Rodríguez Alcalá, Didier T. Jaén, and Enrique Pupo-Walker.[14]

The first reading of *Pedro Páramo* leaves the impression of a disorganized, chaotic structure. The reader does not know if the characters are dead or alive; the speakers with few exceptions are not identified; it is not known if they are thinking or speaking to someone who does not answer; the narrator, Juan Preciado, dies before the middle of the novel; there are constant interruptions of the narrative sequence, numerous points of view, and shifts in time and space without rhetorical transitions. Nevertheless, a careful reading reveals that Rulfo has skillfully structured his novel, not by using the traditional chronological sequence of events which unfolds from past to present with occasional flashbacks, but by giving it a poetic structure in which the many scenes are integrated by the repetition of key images.

The narrative does not formally begin with the arrival of Juan Preciado at Comala at the opening of the novel, but later with the conversation between Juan and Dorotea in their graves, where they are buried together. This interpretation helps the reader to account for the events that take place between the arrival of Juan at Comala and his death two days later. Juan describes his own death with these words, "'I remember seeing something like a cloud of foam, and washing myself in the foam, and losing myself in the cloud. That was the last thing I saw'" (56). In the sequence immediately following his death, his dialogue with Dorotea is revealed for the first time. She answers him saying, "'Are you asking me to believe you died of suffocation, Juan Preciado? I found you in the plaza, a long way from Donis's house. . . . If there wasn't any air on the night you talk about, how did we have the strength to bring you out here and bury you? And you can see that we buried you'" (56). Soon after Juan's death, Dorotea also dies and she is buried with him.

The events occurring during the two days that Juan spends in Comala are really being remembered by him and told to Dorotea in their grave; however, the entire narrative of this first thread is being related by Juan.[15] Other devices are used to retell the stories that were told to him after he arrived at Comala, such as delegated point of view, interior monologue, and dialogues between the souls of the former inhabitants of Comala (Abundio, Dorotea, Eduviges, Damiana, Donis and his sister/wife), all of whom are dead. Rulfo has said that the novel is about a dead town "where no one lives except souls, and even the narrator is dead."[16] Yet, by means of his narrative skills Rulfo gives them all life and makes them live for the reader once more. His problem consists in creating the illusion that these dead people are alive, and at the same time preventing the novel from becoming a realistic account of narrated events. He does this by intermingling motifs and expressions which refer to both this world and the other world. At the very beginning of the novel there is a conversation between Juan Preciado and his guide, the muleteer Abundio, who turns out to be his half-brother. Just before entering Comala, Abundio says that they are almost there. Juan answers:

> "I know. But what about the village? It looks deserted."
> "That isn't how it looks. It is. Nobody lives there any more."
> "And Pedro Páramo?"
> "Pedro Páramo died a long time ago." (5)

Abundio invites Juan to stay with him at his house, which is a little farther on. "But if you want to stay here," he says, "go ahead, even if it's just to take a look at the village. Maybe you'll find somebody living" (6). But he finds only ghosts, dead people. The first soul he meets is that of Eduviges Dyada, who rents rooms to visitors, and whose "face was so pale, you would think there wasn't any blood in her body" (14). Then comes Damiana Cisneros, Juan's old nurse, who visits him at Eduviges's house and tells him, "'Yes, the village is full of echoes. They don't scare me any more. I hear the dogs howling and let them howl, because I know there aren't any dogs here any more. And on windy days you can hear the wind shaking the leaves, but you already know there aren't any trees. There must have been trees here once, or where would the leaves have come from?'" (40). She herself is just a shadow. Juan asks, "'Are you alive, Damiana? Tell me, Damiana! . . . Damiana! Damiana Cisneros!' And the echoes answered me: '. . . Ana . . . neros . . . ! . . . Ana . . . neros . . . !'" (41). Although these dead persons speak, their voices cannot be heard. Juan says, "The words I had heard up till then didn't have any sound, they were silent words you could sense but not hear, like those in a dream" (45).

Finally, there are Donis and his sister/wife, who, with the help of Dorotea, bury Juan when he dies. With his death the narrative thread continues in the grave. But before that, the narration of the experiences of Juan in Comala, told by himself, are constantly interrupted by (1) his own interior monologues and remembered dialogues held with his mother before she died; (2) his observations on the nature of the village; (3) scenes remembered or visualized by one of the other characters, as when Eduviges relates the tragic death of Miguel Páramo; and (4) dialogues between nameless dead villagers.

At the same time, before Juan Preciado dies, the omniscient narrator initiates the second narrative thread, whose subject matter is the life of Pedro Páramo: his dreams as a boy, his love for Susana San Juan, his life in the house of his grandmother, his father's death, his sordid deals to take possession of the land, and his relations with Father Rentería. The narrative devices used here are:

(1) Indirect interior monologues by some of the characters, among them Fulgor Sedano, Pedro Páramo's majordomo. Fulgor comes to see Pedro and is waiting for the door to open: "He knocked with his whip handle at the door of Pedro Páramo's house, and thought of the first time he had knocked there, two weeks earlier" (32). In the monologue that follows, scenes are dramatized and therefore dialogue predominates. To indicate that the monologue has ended (seven pages later), the motif of the whip is repeated: "He knocked again with the handle of his whip, merely to insist, now that he knew they wouldn't open the door till it suited Don Pedro's whim" (39). In the interim between these two knocks, in his long

interior monologue, Fulgor has thought about a number of revealing
incidents illustrating the kind of man Pedro Páramo is.

(2) Direct interior monologues, as when Father Rentería begins to
think to himself while saying mass, " 'There is air and sunlight. There are
white clouds. There is a blue sky, and perhaps there are songs beyond it,
and sweeter voices. . . . There is hope, in a word. There is hope for us in
our suffering. But not for you, Miguel Páramo. You have died in sin and
you can never receive God's grace' " (22). Father Rentería has a good
personal reason to condemn Miguel, as his own niece had been one of the
many girls raped by him.

(3) Conversations among the many *peones* who work for Pedro Páramo.
This affords the author an opportunity to introduce some comic relief.
Speaking about Miguel's death, some *peones* say:

> "This death really hurt me," Terencio Lubianes said. "My shoulders are still
> sore."
> "Mine too," his brother Ubillado said. "And my bunions are twice as big as
> they were before. But the Boss made us all put shoes on . . . and it wasn't even a
> holiday, either. Isn't that right, Toribio?"
> "I don't care what anybody says, I think he died right on time." (26)

The third and last narrative thread is presented from the perspective of
the two persons who have been buried together, Juan and Dorotea. Here
again, there are several points of view, the principal ones being those of
Juan and the omniscient narrator. An important new perspective is
introduced here. Juan and Dorotea can hear the voice of Susana San Juan,
who is buried near them. Structurally, this serves to unite the two worlds
that had remained apart, that of Juan and that of Pedro and Susana. Juan is
now able to hear part of the story directly from Susana's lips: "I'm here,
face up, thinking about those days to forget my loneliness. Because I won't
be lying here for only a little while. And I'm not in my mother's bed, I'm
in a black box, like the coffins they use for burying the dead. Because I'm
dead . . . I remember where I am and I start thinking . . ." (73–74).
Juan, who has heard the voice, says to Dorotea:

> "Was it you that said all that, Dorotea?"
> "What? I was napping for a while. . . ."
> "I heard somebody talking. A woman's voice. I thought it was you."
> "A woman's voice? It must be the one that talks to herself. Doña Susanita.
> She's buried in the big tomb near us. The dampness must have reached her and
> she's turning in her sleep."

"Who is she?"

"Pedro Páramo's last wife. Some people say she's crazy, some say she isn't. The truth is, she talked to herself even when she was alive." (76)

The dialogues between Juan and Dorotea are often interrupted by other voices coming from persons buried nearby. "'What happens to these old corpses,'" Dorotea says to Juan, "'is that when the dampness reaches them they begin to stir. And then they wake up'" (77). The monologues and dialogues of the dead persons are likewise interrupted by the omniscient narrator, who interpolates scenes (as was done in the first thread) but conceals his presence. In the last fragment of the novel, which is not divided into chapters, the death of Pedro Páramo is dramatized. He died as he had lived, thinking about Susana, his unfulfilled love.

Imagery

To integrate the three threads of the novel (which consists of sixty-six fragments), use is made of recurring key images. One of the most important is that of water, which, as a rule, serves as a transition device to bring the reader into the world of Pedro Páramo, but which also gives continuity to scenes that are interrupted by other scenes in a different space or time. The fragment where Pedro Páramo is first introduced, as a boy in his grandmother's house, opens with this motif. "The water that dripped from the roof-tiles was making a hole in the sand in the patio. It fell drip, drip, drip on a laurel leaf, and the leaf bowed down and bobbed up again" (9). Pedro is thinking about Susana when she left the community. "I was thinking of you, Susana. In the green hills. When we flew kites in the windy season" (9). He even remembers that the girl's eyes were moist, "as if they had been kissing the dew," an image that is to be repeated later, just before Pedro's death:

"Susana," he said, and closed his eyes. "I begged you to come back. . . .
". . . There was a full moon overhead. I couldn't stop looking at you. The moonlight bathed your face. I looked and looked at the vision that you were. Soft and shining in the moonlight. Your lips moist and shining with stars. Your body turning transparent in the dew. Susana. Susana San Juan." (122)

Her eyes are also associated to the image of water, this time sea water. "I was remembering you. When you were there looking at me with your sea-green eyes" (10).

That same night that Pedro, as a boy, is remembering Susana, it rains again. Pedro "listened to the drumming of the water for a long while" (12). The next morning it is still drizzling, and Pedro, watching the windowpane, associates the water drops with Susana. He thinks, "I was watching the drops fall, Susana, in the glare of the lightning, and every breath I breathed was a sigh, and every thought was a thought of you" (12).

The water motif is also used to give continuity to other scenes, like the one that takes place in Eduviges's house, where Juan and Eduviges are talking. Their conversation is abruptly interrupted by an episode, introduced by the water image, which transports the reader to Pedro Páramo's world when he was a boy. Eduviges is speaking:

"Have you ever heard the groan of a dead man?" she asked me.
"No, Doña Eduviges."
"You're better off."

The drops fell from the trough, one by one. You could hear the clear water fall from the stone brim into the water jar. (21)

Eight pages later, Eduviges's phrase is repeated. "'You're better off, my son,' Eduviges Dyada told me. 'You're better off,'" and the reader is back with Juan Preciado.

Later, after Juan is buried in his tomb and is listening to Susana, who at this time is first introduced as a character, the water motif is again utilized. The author makes use of a popular belief to give the situation (conversations among dead people) some credibility. It is a common belief among the people of Mexico and other Spanish American countries that when it rains, and the ground becomes wet, dead people wake up.

Susana, in Pedro Páramo's mind, is associated with another image, that of red light. As a boy, Pedro thinks about Susana. "The day you went away, I knew I would never see you again. Your face was dark in the blood-red light of the setting sun" (18) ("'Ibas teñida de rojo por el sol de la tarde, por el crepúsculo ensangrentado del cielo,'" 1955 ed., 27). And after Pedro has lost Susana forever, he says in a loud voice, "'It's been a long time since you left me, Susana. The light was the same as it is now. Not so reddish, but just as weak and cold, because the sun was hidden by the clouds. Everything's the same. It's even the same moment'" (116). Thus, by repeating the same image when the vision of Susana's departure is re-created, and by placing it at the same hour of the day that it took place in the past, time seems to be abolished. This is a literary device that occurs throughout the novel.

Besides serving to integrate the several narrative fragments, these images and a number of others are also utilized for the purpose of identifying the personages with certain natural phenomena, thus giving the characters a deeper significance. Just as Susana's passionate nature is associated with red light, Miguel Páramo's fiery nature brings forth the image of falling stars. The night when he was buried, "there were falling stars. They fell as if the sky were raining fire" (27). After this passage the star motif is repeated to serve as a transition to the world of Father Rentería, who blames himself for Miguel's immoral behavior and for having forgiven him:

> There were falling stars. The lights of Comala went out one by one, and the sky took possession of the night.
> Father Rentería turned in his bed, unable to sleep. Everything that happened is my fault, he told himself. Afraid to offend the people who have money. (28)

Later, Father Rentería is thinking about the night Miguel had died. "Many years later, Father Rentería still remembered the night . . . Miguel Páramo died. He wandered through the solitary streets of Comala. . . . When he came to the river he stopped there beside the calm water, watching the reflections of the stars that fell from heaven (66–67).

The wind is another of the recurring motifs found in the novel. It is first associated with Juan's mother, Dolores Preciado. She also brings to mind the color and brightness of nature. When Juan reaches Comala, he remembers his mother's description of the place. " 'Green fields. You can see the horizon rise and fall when the wind moves in the wheat, or when the rain ruffles it in the afternoon. The color of the earth, the smell of alfalfa and bread. A village that smells of new honey . . .' " (16). After Juan is dead, he keeps recalling his mother's words, " 'You'll see why I loved it there, my son. The village I loved. . . . Full of trees and green leaves, . . . always the same except for the difference in the air. The air changes the colors of everything . . .' " (56).

The image of the gray sky is associated in Pedro Páramo's mind with the death of his father, who was killed at dawn, when the sky was still gray. When Pedro was still a boy, his mother came to his room, stood at the door, and gave him the tragic news. At that moment "there were no stars, only a leaden sky, not cleared yet by the shining of the sun" (22). This moment is engraved permanently in Pedro Páramo's memory, and many years later, in the same room and on a similar morning, he remembers the scene. Again, time stands still.

The *arrayán* ("myrtle," or "bayberry") is an image that appears twice, first when Miguel Páramo takes advantage of Ana, Father Rentería's niece, and later to stress the bitter nature of the environment around Comala. In a conversation between the priest of Contla (a neighboring town) and Father Rentería, the priest makes a remark to illustrate the perverse nature of the Páramo clan. "'We live in a region where everything is given us, thanks to Providence, but where everything is bitter. That's what we're condemned to.'" Father Rentería agrees and says, "'You're right. I've tried to raise grapes in Comala. They don't bear. Only oranges and berries. Bitter oranges and bitter berries'" (70; "Naranjos agrios y arrayanes agrios" in the Spanish ed., 1959, 89). The implication is that the good land, Paradise, has been turned into a bitter land by man's transgressions, for which the Páramo family serves as a metaphor.[17]

Animal motifs play an important part in the structure of the novel. The horse and the bull are both used to stress the virile characteristics of Pedro Páramo and his son Miguel. There is a close association between Miguel and his horse. Eduviges, when talking to Juan Preciado, turns her head slightly as if listening to a distant sound. When Juan asks her what she hears, she shakes her head and says, "'It's just that horse of his, coming and going the way it does. They were inseparable. It runs everywhere looking for him, and it always comes back at this hour'" (19).

The bull, also a symbol of *machismo*, is associated with Pedro Páramo. Early one morning he visits *la chacha (muchacha)* Margarita, a servant in his hacienda. Damiana, who lives nearby, hears Pedro's knocking and gets up just in time to see him climbing through Margarita's window. "The bulls were lowing far off in the darkness. 'Those animals never sleep,' Damiana Cisneros said. 'Never. They're like the devil himself, who's always looking for souls to take down to Hell'" (103).[18]

An important motif used in the novel is that composed of two mythical images, the evening star and the moon. This is natural since an early title of the novel was to have been "Una estrella junto a la luna" [A star near the moon]. This motif is appropriately associated to the brother and sister who live as man and wife in a shack in Comala. The shack is made up of a single room with a broken roof through which the sky can be seen. Juan, who is staying with the couple on his second night in Comala, can see the evening star appear after darkness descends, followed later by the moon. When an old woman, who is more like a ghost than a human, comes into the room, Juan is terrified and cannot move. Finally he is able to turn his head and look "over there where the evening star was shining next to the moon" (52). This motif has its origin in ancient Nahuatl mythology. According to the Toltec myth, the god Quetzalcóatl descended to the underworld to ask the god Mictlantecuhtli for the bones of the dead in order to create a new man. There is a suggested association, in the novel, between Quetzalcóatl and Juan Preciado brought about by the motif of the evening star, or Venus, with which the god was identified. Juan, too, descended into Comala in search of the dead. And, like Quetzalcóatl, who had to descend to the underworld after he had committed the carnal act, Juan dies, after sleeping with Donis's sister. The Toltec myth symbolized the passing of the planet Venus below the horizon and its reappearance as the morning star. The moon, on the other hand, is often associated with the god Tezcatlipoca, the symbol of death, evil, and destruction, as well as Quetzalcóatl's enemy and conqueror. The association of Pedro Páramo with the moon motif is revealed by the name of his hacienda, Media Luna ("Half Moon"). The coming together of Venus and the moon, as seen by Juan, represents, as it did to the ancient Mexicans, the struggle between life and death. Therefore, Rulfo's novel, by means of this motif, becomes a metaphor of that struggle.

Chapter Seven
El gallo de oro and Other Writings
Introduction

In March 1980, Editorial Era of Mexico City published a new book by Juan Rulfo, *El gallo de oro y otros textos para cine* [The golden cock and other scripts]. Many of Rulfo's readers had been expecting to see his much-publicized novel "La cordillera" or his collection of short stories "Días sin floresta,"[1] but neither of these has come off the press as yet. Instead, he has published a collection of movie scripts under the title of the longest of them, *El gallo de oro,* a small book of only 134 pages. There is an Introduction by Jorge Ayala Blanco, and the Editorial Era thanks Pablo Rulfo (Juan Rulfo's son), Rubén Gámez, and Antonio Reynoso for their invaluable help in the publishing of the book. It is not clear, however, what part each had in the preparation of the manuscript, or to what extent the author himself collaborated in the publishing of the book.

In the Introduction Ayala Blanco states that the book brings together the main piece, *El gallo de oro;* the screen narative for *El despojo,* a twelve-minute short subject directed in 1960 by Antonio Reynoso and photographed in black and white by Corkidi; and two pieces written by Rulfo for *La fórmula secreta,* a forty-two-minute movie directed and photographed by Rubén Gámez in 1964. It seems that one of these two pieces was written *a posteriori,* and the other with the purpose of interpreting the movie to the public.

El gallo de oro

The title piece, *El gallo de oro,* is a novelette of eighty pages which was made into a movie in 1964 by the well-known director Roberto Gavaldón. The film appeared at an inappropriate time, for in 1964 the Mexican cinema was undergoing a change of direction. A group of young directors had been experimenting with new techniques and introducing new sub-

90

ject matter in an attempt to revitalize an industry that had become complacent as a result of its great success in the Spanish-speaking world with its numerous *películas rancheras,* based on song and folklore.[2]

Rulfo had written *El gallo de oro* during the early 1960s for Manuel Barbachano Ponce, producer of such successful films as *Raíces* (1954), *Torero* (1956), and *Nazarín* (1958), among others. From Rulfo's narrative the script for the movie was prepared by two prominent novelists, Carlos Fuentes and Gabriel García Márquez, the latter then living in Mexico. According to Ayala Blanco, "although Roberto Gavaldón filmed the movie in 1964, giving Rulfo the corresponding credits, the results were far removed from the original, still waiting to be faithfully transformed into a movie."[3] Film critics were not at all enthusiastic about Gavaldón's film. José de la Colina compared it to Luis Alcoriza's *Tarahumara* (1961), stating that the latter film provides "a possible model for Mexican commercial movies, which is not true of the pompous, spectacular, folklorish products which, although endowed with minimal intellectual and aesthetic pretentiousness, reflect the old formulas of the quaint cinema, as in the case of Ricardo Gavaldón's *El gallo de oro.*"[4] One of these films belonging to what De la Colina calls "quaint cinema" is *Ánimas Trujano* (1960 or 1961), based on the novel *La mayordomía* (1952) by Rogelio Barriga Rivas, and which doubtless had influence over Gavaldón when filming *El gallo de oro.*

The anonymous review of the film *El gallo de oro* published in the weekly news magazine *Tiempo* was much more severe. It was called "a film really representative of the old cinema which tries to cover up its obsolescence. On the negative side, it encloses the roots of the folklorish school that the contemporary Mexican cinema has destroyed." Nevertheless, conscious of the fact that the narrative was written by Rulfo and the script by Fuentes and García Márquez, three famous novelists, the critic adds, "The narrative expression is decorous and, to a certain degree, modern."[5]

The problem to be determined is whether Rulfo wrote *El gallo de oro* as a novel or as a film narrative. If as a film, it is natural that he would have placed it in the hands of the producer; if as a novel, why wasn't it published after it was written, in the 1960s or, perhaps, even earlier? What Rulfo said in Guadalajara, in June 1962, two years before the film appeared, may shed some light on the matter. He called this work *El gallero* and not *El gallo de oro,* and said, "I completed this novel but did not publish it because they asked me for a movie script and since the work had many folkloric elements, I believed it could easily be adapted to a movie. I myself wrote the script. However, when I presented it they told me it had numerous elements that could not be used. . . . The artistic materials I destroyed. Now it is impossible for me to reconstruct them."[6] *El gallo de oro,* as published in 1980, does not have the form of a film script; it is a novelette. The narrative technique used is one for a work to be read. The use of the omniscient narrator, with his descriptions of nature, comments about the characters, and judgments regarding their actions, is a technique used by the novelist and not by the script writer. In one of the novel's scenes the principal characters, Dionisio Pinzón, Bernarda Cutiño, and Lorenzo Benavides, are sitting at a table in a café in one of the many villages they visit while following the carnivals. Bernarda advises Dionisio regarding a business deal, "Go ahead and accept his proposal, *gallero* ["professional cockfighter"], it is to your advantage." The omniscient narrator interrupts the dialogue to say, "said La Caponera [Bernarda], who was sitting facing Pinzón" (45). It would not be necessary to inform a movie audience of this kind of directional information, but a novelist would certainly need to avail his readers of it.

However, in the novel, as in the movie, folkloric elements predominate. The characters, ambience, scenes, and images are all drawn from Mexican folklore; more specifically, from the folklore of Jalisco; and above all, from the lore related to cockfighting as practiced in the Bajío region of Central Mexico. In this sense, *El gallo de oro* is a regional novelette. The protagonist, Dionisio Pinzón, first appears as a poor town crier, representing a popular character in Mexican folklore whose presence in the villages goes back to the Colonial period. He becomes a cockfighter and later a gambler, two professions closely associated with the folk tradition. His wife, Bernarda Cutiño, "called La Caponera ["The Lead Mare"], because, perhaps, of the pull she had with men" (26), is a carnival singer, a profession handed down from generation to generation. Her mother had been a carnival singer, and her own daughter will follow in this profession. Other characters (Lorenzo Benavides and Secundino Colmenero) are also cockfighters.

The fact that Bernarda is a singer gives the writer an opportunity to introduce popular songs in his work, and Rulfo does not disappoint the reader, for she sings some folk songs taken from the rich musical tradition for which Jalisco is famous. The songs, however, are not used merely to give the novel a popular flavor, as is common in the *ranchera film,* but rather to characterize the personages who sing these songs and to reflect their sentiments. Before marrying Dionisio, Bernarda reveals her love for him by means of one of the many songs she sings in the cockpit. "While Dionisio Pinzón was looking for a vacant seat she went up to the stage and from there began to sing" (52–53). The song she sings, reproduced in part, uses the imagery of the native cacti, the pitahaya, and the garambullo, and includes these verses:

> Although I may go
> My heart stays with you.

This encourages Dionisio, who not long after that marries La Caponera.

The world in which the *galleros* move in the novel is that of the small towns of El Bajío in Central Mexico—Teocaltiche, Aguascalientes, Arandas, Zacatecas, Tlaquepaque. It is the world of the village fiestas, which have almost disappeared. Here the reader finds the professional roulette, card, and dice gamblers; the popular *corrido* and *ranchera* singers; the mariachi players, and the many independent circus performers. Most important of all, there are the cock fights. When the fiesta was celebrated in Dionisio's town, San Miguel del Milagro, he was hired by the *galleros* to announce the fights. The last fight one night was fought between a golden cock from Chihuahua and a white one from Chicontepec. The white rooster was much inferior, yet, as the result of a lucky break, he won, wounding the golden cock, which was the favorite. Its owner was going to finish him off, but Dionisio asked him for it and was lucky enough to get it. He nursed the golden cock back to a fighting condition and became a *gallero.* Thus he was able to marry La Caponera, a woman who brings luck to whoever is her companion. When the golden cock is finally killed, Dionisio for a moment loses his confidence. "Dionisio Pinzón left the cockpit carrying in his hands a few feathers and a memory of blood. Outside, the roaring of the carnival could be heard: the amusements, the barkers, the lottery game, the roulette, the low-pitched voices of the card and dice players, and the high-pitched voices of those who invited the on-lookers to try and guess where the hidden ball was" (48–49). Dionisio cannot abandon all this, so he continues as a *gallero,* but soon becomes a gambler. Bernarda brings him luck as long as she is near him, so he cannot lose. He becomes quite rich, and sets up a gambling casino in the huge ranch he has bought. However, Bernarda dies while he is gambling, and he loses everything. His only way out is suicide.

After the death of Dionisio and Bernarda, their daughter is forced to earn a living by singing at the fairs as her mother did, thus giving the narrative a circular structure and, at the same time, bringing together the principal guide lines by which the personages are ruled:

A few days later that girl, who had had everything, and who now had nothing but her voice to earn her a living, was singing from a stage at the cockpit of Cocotlán, a forgotten town in one of Mexico's most isolated regions. She was singing like her mother began to sing during her days, expressing in her songs all the deep feelings caused by her helplessness. (101)

The tragic note characteristic of Rulfo's narratives is found in the lives of Dionisio and Bernarda; in Dionisio because of his inability to harmonize his inner life with his desire to be wealthy. To attain his goal he exploits Bernarda's power to bring him good luck, and although he still loves her, she becomes a mere instrument in his life. When she dies, sitting in the darkness behind a shade in his gambling room, Dionisio loses everything he has, including his life. And even after her death he blames Bernarda for not having warned him of her poor health. When they are buried, she is taken to the cemetery "in a black coffin made in a hurry out of the cheapest wood. And he, in a gray coffin with silver trimmings" (100).

Bernarda's tragedy is the result of her almost magical power to bring good luck to those who accompany her. As a feminine symbol, Bernarda represents the opposite of the *femme fatale*. Her gift, however, brings her misfortune, since the men she loves return her love only because of the power that she possesses. Her desire to be free, which compels her to follow the fairs in her profession as a singer in spite of the fact that Dionisio is very rich, comes to an end when she loses her voice. She had been able to escape Benavides, only to fall into the hands of Dionisio, for whom she becomes an amulet for the rest of her life. Her longing for liberty is reborn in her daughter, who manages to keep her freedom from male dominance. In one of her songs she gives expression to that feeling:

> Si te quise no fue que te quise
> si te amé, fue por pasar el rato,
> hay [ahí] te mando tu triste retrato
> para nunca acordarme de ti. . . . (39)

> (If I loved you it was make believe
> If I loved you it was just a pastime.
> I'm sending you back your sad, sad portrait
> To get you forever out of my mind.)

Although it lacks depth, *El gallo de oro* is characteristic of Rulfo. And while it does not reach the heights attained with *Pedro Páramo* or *El llano en llamas,* its world is the same, tragic and resigned. If there are technical, structural, and stylistic defects, the novel nevertheless presents Rulfo's characteristic interpretation of Mexican reality, which he knows so well. In the development of Mexican narrative, it represents the best treatment of the place of the *gallero* and cockfighting in the world of popular entertainment.

El despojo

El despojo [The plunder] was filmed in 1960 by Antonio Reynoso during weekends, without a fully prepared script, and using nonprofessional actors. It was photographed by Rafael Corkidi and followed a plot made up by Rulfo, who also prepared the dialogues. The action is set in the Valle del Mezquital in the state of Hidalgo, one of the most desolated regions in the Republic of Mexico. It is in this same valley that Mauricio Magdaleno's novel *El resplandor*[7] (1937) takes place. The short Rulfo script of five pages is a series of ten numbered sequences consisting of stage directions and dialogues. There are three personages, Pedro, Don Celerino, and Petra. In the first sequence the Indian Pedro, carrying a large guitar, is on his way to the nearby village. He stops to rest and begins to reflect. Offstage the voice of Pedro is heard saying that he has resolved to prevent Don Celerino, who has already dispossessed him of his land and home, from taking his wife, Petra. "And if they kill me, what does it matter. After all, for some time now I have lost all desire to keep on living. It is all right if he takes my land and my house, but my wife, never! I shall take her with me far away, forever" (109).

The second sequence takes place in the village where Pedro comes across Don Celerino, "an influential and fierce-looking mestizo" (110). Pedro shoots him, but before Don Celerino dies he shoots back and kills Pedro. In the film Pedro's image freezes, but the action continues. There seems to be no doubt that the short story "An Occurrence at Owl Creek Bridge" by Ambrose Bierce influenced Rulfo in the writing of this script. In Bierce's story the protagonist, Peyton Farquhar, a northern Alabama planter, continues to live after having been hanged by federal soldiers on a scaffold set on a loose plank on the bridge at Owl Creek. It is implied that the rope broke and that he fell into the river, escaped, and went back home to his wife. However, at the end of the story it is revealed that all the action surrounding his escape took place in Farquhar's mind before he died.[8] The same technique was used by Jorge Luis Borges in his story "El milagro secreto" except that the protagonist, a writer by the name of Jaromir Hladík, faced a firing squad.[9]

In the third sequence of Rulfo's script, Pedro arrives at his *jacal* ("hut")
and tells Petra that he has killed Don Celerino and orders her to get ready
to flee. In this dialogue it is revealed that Pedro's son, Lencho, had been
badly beaten while trying to defend his mother, and he cannot walk.
Sequences four to nine depict the flight through the *llano*, with Pedro
carrying his dying son in his arms. Upon leaving the village they believe a
malignant spirit, a *nahual*, has crossed their path. The *llano* they must
cross is very much like that found in the story "Nos han dado la tierra,"
desolated, dry, and eroded. Pedro tries to encourage his son by telling him
that at the end of the *llano* "the earth is so green that even the sky is green.
There no one will bother you. There you will be able to play around
without fear of being stung by thorns or bitten by snakes" (112). But the
boy dies and is buried in the middle of the *llano*. In the last sequence the
action returns to sequence two, with Pedro falling over his huge guitar
which emits a strident sound and breaks into a thousand pieces.

This short composition is typical of Rulfo's writing in the thematic
treatment of death, revenge, and despoilment. It is at the same time a
protest against the *cacique* system which still prevails in rural Mexico,
where the local boss rules over the lives of the people, especially the Indian,
not unlike what the conquistadors and *encomenderos* did during the Colonial
period.

La fórmula secreta

In 1964 Rubén Gámez directed and photographed the experimental
film *La fórmula secreta* using a text by Rulfo in two of the ten sequences. In
black and white, the film lasts forty-two minutes and is made up of ten
unrelated sequences, some of which deal with the Americanization of
Mexican life. The two sequences accompanied by Rulfo's text, however,
treat of the relations between man and his environment. They depict man's
inability to make a living from the earth and, while he might survive, he
goes through life forever hungry. Hunger is, indeed, the central theme of
this poetic prose, read for the film by the poet Jaime Sabines. Although the
two sequences with Rulfo's commentaries do not appear consecutively,
they deal with the same theme. The scenery resembles a Martian landscape, full of crevices, among which appear farmers looking intensely at
the camera. They seem to be part of the rocky landscape, symbolizing
petrified human life.

It is difficult to determine from this text what Rulfo's original composition was like, since here it is reproduced (apparently transcribed from the
film) as rhythmic prose.

> Cola de relámpago,
>   remolino de muertos.
> Con el vuelo que llevan,
>   poco les durará el esfuerzo. (123)
>
> (Lightning's tail,
>   death's whirlwind.
> With that momentum,
>   short your effort will be).

According to Ayala Blanco, the idea of giving Rulfo's prose a rhythmic form came from Carlos Monsiváis when the first version was published in the 30 March 1976 number of *La Cultura en México,* the literary supplement of the weekly *Siempre!* For the second version, appearing in *El gallo de oro* (121–25), the help of the poet José Emilio Pacheco was sought.[10]

The Secret Formula was released in 1965, and to help the public understand the nature of the film Rulfo was asked to write some program notes which were distributed, appearing anonymously, the first day the film was shown at the Regis movie house in Mexico City in November 1965. In this note, entitled "Sinopsis," Rulfo informs the public that the ten apparently unrelated episodes have a central theme, and although dissimilar, attain unity by being presented as the product of a mind under stress. A man in the hospital is in need of a blood transfusion. He is given a transfusion with a liquid made from a secret formula (Coca-Cola?) which produces visions in his mind of a world in the shape of a tunnel where misery, pain, poverty, anguish, and panic predominate. United by that framing tale, the unrelated, short episodes present a tragic view of contemporary Mexico. Although only two of the episodes are the product of Rulfo's imagination, the rest do not clash with his view of the world.

The other narrative texts which Rulfo prepared for two films, *Paloma herida* [Wounded dove, 1962] and *En este pueblo no hay ladrones* [There are no thieves in this town, 1964], have not been published. The first, lasting one hour and twenty minutes, was directed by Emilio Fernández. The second, directed by Alberto Isaac, is of interest because Rulfo himself has a part in the movie as an actor, alongside Carlos Monsiváis and the director.

Nonfiction Writings

In addition to his fiction, Rulfo has published a few essays, book reviews, and articles. He has also given a number of interviews and lectures that have appeared in print. Reina Roffé collected all of the statements made by Rulfo in these interviews and published them in December 1972 under his own name with the title *Autobiografía armada* [A reconstructed autobiography].[11] The material is arranged in such a manner that it appears to have been written by the author since there are no editorial intrusions, and interviewers' names and questions have been omitted. It is not stated whether this book was published with the consent of Rulfo; nevertheless, the work gives a complete picture of Rulfo's life and his opinions regarding his own works as well as comments on a number of subjects, especially literature.

On 21 August 1965, Rulfo gave a lecture on the novel at the Instituto de Ciencias y Artes de Chiapas, which was later published.[12] More recently (1974) he talked extensively about his own works with students at the Universidad Central de Venezuela in a dialogue which was also published.[13] In 1980, upon being admitted to the Mexican Academy of Letters, he read a study on the life and works of the Mexican poet José Gorostiza, whose seat he now occupies.[14]

There is no question as to where Rulfo's interest lies as a literary critic. He is mainly preoccupied with the novel, almost to the total exclusion of other genres. His knowledge of world fiction has been amply documented. In his study on the novel Rulfo not only considers that of his own country, but also the novels of Europe, the United States, and Latin America. His longest study of a single novel is the one dedicated to Agustín Yáñez's *La tierra pródiga* [The prodigal land].[15] In this study Rulfo explores the historical background of the novel, which treats of the struggle for power in a region of Jalisco (Valle de Expuchimilco) called, by Yáñez, "the prodigal land." It was reserved for Yáñez, Rulfo states, to dramatize that struggle by creating characters like Ricardo Guerra, the protagonist, who are representative of the people who have lived there since the Colonial period. Rulfo ends his study with an evaluation of Yáñez's novel, which he considers to be one of the greatest works of Mexican fiction, for with it the author was able to expose the true nature of the rulers of that rich section of the state which has been devastated by greed and the struggle for power.

In his lecture on the novel, Rulfo stated that he would concentrate on the European and the American novels, since these are the novels best known in our time. He began by saying that since World War II there has been almost a complete change of direction in the writing of fiction. Before the war, according to Rulfo, the novel published in the United States was the most important. William Faulkner, John Steinbeck, and other American writers influenced European writers, but later Europe was to be the source of innovation. The American influence was felt especially in Italy.

Alberto Moravia, one of the earlier writers, replaced his popular novels with a new type of fiction. The influence of the later Italian novelists— Vasco Pratolini, Elio Vittorini, Italo Calvino, Cesare Pavese—extended to other European countries, the United States, and Latin America. Their contribution to Italian fiction was the elimination of dialect. Pratolini, especially, with his novel *A Tale of Poor Lovers* (translated 1949), advanced considerably European narrative fiction. Rulfo states that Calvino is the best novelist of the group. He does seem to regret, however, that most of them chose the theme of frustration for their novels. He also regrets the lack of action in some novels of writers such as Pavese and Carlo Cassola. Having in mind Cassola's *Il Soldato* [The soldier, translated 1967] he says: "They write but it seems that they are not describing anything; nothing ever happens to their personages. The reader asks himself, 'Well, what has happened?'"[16] Nevertheless, he admires the novelists' skill in maintaining the interest of the reader. "It is worth observing," he adds, "how something leading nowhere is able to keep the attention of the reader. Nevertheless, that seems to be the destiny of contemporary letters."[17]

Of the French novelists, Rulfo admires those who have revolted against the formality of the Academy, as did Jean Giono. "Any author that revolts against the Academy," he says, "is ignored and a conspiracy of silence unfolds around him. That's what happened, for example, to Jean Giono, a writer who continues to be relevant, but who for many years remained unrecognized. The same thing happened to [Charles-Ferdinand] Ramuz, a native of the French region of Switzerland."[18]

Rulfo is very frank about his dislike of the so-called antinovelists. "To write antinovels," he says, "is precisely to avoid all thinking, only to see, and to explain what is being observed."[19] He does, however, admire some of the writers of antinovels, among them Michel Butor and Nathalie Sarraute. It seems that the novels of Alain Robbe-Grillet do not appeal to him. On the other hand, he does reserve a great deal of admiration for a German novelist, Günter Grass, especially for his novels *The Tin Drum* (translated 1962) and *Cat and Mouse* (translated 1963). *"The Tin Drum,"* he says, "opens to the novel immense possibilities. It is the opposite of the antinovel. It demonstrates that it is possible to write a novel and that it is not necessary to get to the point of the antinovel."[20] Other German novelists Rulfo seems to like are Uwe Johnson and the Swiss-Germans Max Frisch and Friedrich Dürrenmatt.

Rulfo dedicated the rest of his lecture to the American novel after Faulkner, giving some attention to J. D. Salinger, William Styron, Norman Mailer, Truman Capote, John Updike, Jack Kerouac, and Joseph

Heller. He considers Heller "one of the best North American writers."[21] In general, however, Rulfo believes that the new American novel has not surpassed the achievements obtained by Sherwood Anderson, William Faulkner, and James T. Farrell.

It is well known that Rulfo is a great admirer of the Nordic novelists, some of whom have influenced him. He regrets, and this contradicts his own preference as a writer of fiction, that the followers of Knut Hamsun lack the happiness that characterizes his fiction, "that great happiness that gives man a truly human nature."[22] Rulfo dedicates the last pages of his lecture to a brief discussion of the contemporary novel in England, Hungary, Czechoslovakia, and Yugoslavia. In his concluding remarks he gives his opinion as to what a novel should cover. According to him, a novel should encompass an imagined reality, without apparent relation to life as we know it. It is not demanded of the novelist that he "experience life," but that he discover that which cannot be seen by the eye; that he make use of his instincts more than his senses; that he use intuition more than perception, *"conocer más que saber."*[23] "Realism," he says, "we can get hold of; but not magic, which is inside each one of us."[24] With those words Rulfo ends his revealing survey of the contemporary novel.

On 13 March 1974, Rulfo was invited by the Central University of Venezuela to participate in a dialogue with students. The results of that interchange were published in 1976 in the periodical *Escritura* with the title "Juan Rulfo Examines His Narrative." Although he repeated much of what he had said earlier, he did add new information regarding his own works. He also repeated that he had been influenced by the Nordic novelists, and added, "I have always liked Nordic literature because it gives the impression of a misty, hazy environment. . . . I like very much what is sad, what is sad and nebulous."[25]

Of interest also is the answer he gave regarding magical realism. Having been asked his opinion about that literary trend, he said with great frankness, "I do not yet know what magical realism is, as I do not know either what socialist realism is, but I believe that the term was invented to say that reality is transformed into myth, or that reality and myth are interwoven. It seems that Miguel Ángel Asturias was the inventor of that term. I believe García Márquez has been the one who has utilized that theory more in his writing, with very good results. But I do not know, up to this moment, what magical realism is."[26]

Rulfo's nonfiction writings, although few, are of interest not only because they reveal his ideas about literature, especially the novel, but also for what they reveal about Rulfo himself.

Chapter Eight
Concluding Remarks

The works of Juan Rulfo analyzed here present a unity unmatched in Mexican fiction. His three major works deal with the countryside of his native region, the southern, bare, arid, economically and spiritually deprived part of the state of Jalisco where he was born and spent his early years. In both his short stories and novels all of the characters belong to a rural class composed of *campesinos* and *patrones,* living under a social structure inherited from the Spanish Colonial period, but now in a state of transition due first to the social Revolution of 1910 and then to the religious uprising of 1926, which affected and uprooted the population of central Mexico. Rulfo himself experienced this upheaval as a boy, and the impressions left upon his mind were later permanently transformed into aesthetic expression.

To relate these experiences in the form of literary fiction he has made use of three devices: a new narrative technique, a new language, and a tragic world-view. The first he accomplishes by utilizing distorted, spatial, and mythical structures. This technique relates his fiction to the world narrative tradition established by Joyce, Proust, Lawrence, and Faulkner, and establishes him as the initiator of one of several new narrative trends in Latin America.

The second innovation he accomplishes by creating a new narrative style based on the popular speech of the people of Jalisco which he elevates to a literary level characterized by economy of expression, by a starkness reflecting that area and its people, by the use of imagery that gives the language a poetic undertone, and by the employment of a vocabulary, rhythm, and syntax that is peculiarly Mexican. The latter has been singled out by another famous novelist from Jalisco, Agustín Yáñez, as representative of what he considers to be a truly Mexican style based more on its syntax than on the use of Mexicanisms.

Rulfo's tragic world-view is the result of personal experiences, both in his native Jalisco and in Mexico City. He has been able to transform these experiences into stories and novels in which the reader finds a violent, often primitive world. His characters have to struggle against an environment that is never hospitable, an earth from which a living has to be eked out by constant labor and sacrifice. It is a world where life and death complement each other, and where death often triumphs and conquers and dominates the living. And yet, this world vision rises to become a metaphor of the destiny of mankind, not only in rural Mexico, but also in the predominantly rural world of the countries forming the Third World.

Unlike other successful Latin American new novelists, Rulfo has chosen to remain in his own country, where he has become the symbol of that literature that has its roots in the native soil. He has not, like other writers, abandoned the nativist tradition characteristic of the Spanish American novelist of the previous generation. He has, however, by the use of new narrative techniques and a new world vision, transformed that *criollista* tradition into something new, into a fiction that best represents Latin American reality. And although his fiction is basically realistic, as many critics have observed, he has infused into it a magic element that lifts it to the level of the unreal, to the point where a critic might even classify it as fantastic.

It is the combination of a native subject matter observed from a new perspective and expressed by means of up-to-date techniques that has given Rulfo an international status as an extraordinary fiction writer, in spite of the fact that his production is quite limited. And it is his sensitive, poetic vision of his own world that has elevated him to the ranks of the great interpreters of Mexican reality. His fiction has endured the test of time, and it stands as a monument to a modest, sincere, and unobtrusive writer.

Notes and References

(All translations from Spanish sources are mine, unless otherwise stated.)

Chapter One

1. For the literature of this period see José Emilio Pacheco, *Antología del modernismo, 1884–1921* (México: UNAM, 1970); John S. Brushwood, "La novela mexicana frente al porfirismo," *Historia Mexicana* 7 (1958):368–405; Donald L. Schmidt, "The Novelization of Class Consciousness During the *Porfiriato,*" *Latin American Literary Review* 6 (1977):43–52.

2. Alejandro Avilés, "Juan Rulfo opina sobre nuestra novela," *Diorama de la Cultura,* Sunday Supplement of *Excélsior,* Mexico City, 8 June 1969, p. 1.

3. Ibid.

4. Ramón López Velarde, "La suave patria," in *Poesías completas y El minutero* (México: Editorial Porrúa, 1963), p. 270.

5. The opera singer José Mojica was born in San Gabriel in 1896 and spent the early years of his life there, like Rulfo. The town is described in the first few chapters of his autobiography, *Yo pecador* (México: Editorial Jus, 1956).

6. Luis Harss and Barbara Dohmann, "Juan Rulfo, or the Souls of the Departed," in *Into the Mainstream* (New York, 1967), p. 248.

7. Ibid., p. 250. See also "Juan Rulfo," in *Los narradores ante el público* (México: Joaquín Mortiz, 1966), p. 25.

8. María Teresa Gómez Gleason, "Juan Rulfo y el mundo de su próxima novela *La cordillera,*" in *Recopilación de textos sobre Juan Rulfo* (Habana, 1969), p. 150. This article was taken from *Siempre!* (Mexico City), no. 679 (29 June 1966). It also appears in *Juan Rulfo, autobiografía armada,* ed. Reina Roffé (Buenos Aires, 1973), p. 29.

9. Elena Poniatowska, "El terrón de tepetate" [The lump of clay], in *Palabras cruzadas* [Exchanged words] (México: Ediciones Era, 1961), pp. 138–39.

10. Patrick Romanell, *Making of the Mexican Mind* (Notre Dame, Indiana: University of Notre Dame Press, 1971), p. 98.

11. Avilés, "Juan Rulfo," p. 4.

12. *Constitución política de los Estados Unidos Mexicanos* (México: Partido Revolucionario Institucional, 1958), p. 27.

13. Ibid., p. 109.

14. Harss and Dohmann, "Juan Rulfo," p. 252.

15. Roffé, *Juan Rulfo,* p. 46.

16. *Los narradores ante el público,* p. 26. This statement may indicate that Rulfo's father was born in 1892, if he was thirty-three in 1925. Or it may be that Rulfo is just playing with the number thirty-three, the age of Christ when he was crucified.

17. Interview with Juan Rulfo by Ricardo Cortés Tamayo in *Diorama de la Cultura,* Sunday Supplement of *Excélsior,* 31 May 1959, p. 4. Harss, however, states, "The war, which was born in the highlands, in the state of Guanajuato, lasted three years, until 1928. By then it had extended to Rulfo's area. In the very first days of the war he lost his father. Six years later he lost his mother" (252). This would place the death of Rulfo's mother in 1932, the year he left the orphan's school, and is contrary to what Rulfo says in the above quotations.

18. Roffé, *Juan Rulfo,* p. 47.

19. Harss and Dohmann, "Juan Rulfo," p. 253.

20. See Hellén Ferro, "The New Novel of Mexico: A Look at Juan Rulfo," *Americas* 16, no. 10 (October 1964):41.

21. Roffé, *Juan Rulfo,* pp. 49–50.

22. Harss and Dohmann, "Juan Rulfo," p. 253.

23. Roffé, *Juan Rulfo,* p. 50.

24. See Arthur Ramírez, "Style and Technique in Juan Rulfo" (Ph.D. diss., University of Texas, 1973), p. 13.

25. See Manuel Ferrer Chivite, *El laberinto mexicano en/de Juan Rulfo* (México, 1972), p. 22.

26. Roffé, *Juan Rulfo,* p. 52.

27. Marco Antonio Millán, "*América*—Revista Antológica," *Las revistas literarias de México,* Segunda Serie (México: Instituto Nacional de Bellas Artes, 1963), pp. 127–28.

28. Harss and Dohmann, "Juan Rulfo," p. 253.

29. A copy of these program notes is in my possession.

30. *Juan Rulfo: homenaje nacional* (México, 1980).

31. Harss and Dohmann, "Juan Rulfo," p. 254.

32. For these and other translations see Arthur Ramírez, "Hacia una bibliografía de y sobre Juan Rulfo," *Revista Iberoamericana* 11, no. 86 (January–March, 1974):135–71, and also Nila Gutiérrez Marrone's bibliography in her book *El estilo de Juan Rulfo: estudio lingüístico* (New York, 1978).

33. See Bambi, "'La cordillera': nuevo libro de Juan Rulfo," *Excélsior,* 16 April 1963, pp. 4-A, 5-A; also A.S., "Ayuquila, Dionisio Arias, una casta condenada: 'La cordillera,'" *La Gaceta* (del Fondo de Cultura Económica), 11° Suplemento, Primer Trimestre de 1964, p. 6.

34. *Los narradores ante el público,* p. 24.

35. Harss and Dohmann, "Juan Rulfo," p. 274.

36. For a summary of the problem about this unpublished novel see Donald K. Gordon, "Juan Rulfo's Elusive Novel: 'La cordillera,'" *Hispania* 56 (1973):1040–41, and John D. Bruce-Novoa, "Some Answers about Rulfo's 'La cordillera,'" *Hispania* 57 (1974):474–76.

37. Juan Cervera, "Entrevista con Juan Rulfo," *La Gaceta* (del Fondo de Cultura Económica) 15, no. 8 (October 1968):11.

38. As reported by *Tiempo,* 30 Nov. 1970. See also Boyd G. Carter, "Juan Rulfo recibe el Premio Nacional de Letras," *Hispania* 54 (1971):380. For other comments see Ramírez's bibliography, pp. 146–48.

39. See *Excélsior,* Section B, 27 September 1980.

40. Félix Luna, "Imagen de Juan Rulfo," *Clarín Literario* (Buenos Aires), 6 January 1972, p. 7.

41. Hellén Ferro, "New Novel," p. 41.

42. Juan Rulfo, "Situación de la novela contemporánea," *Instituto de Ciencias y Artes de Chiapas* (ICACH) 15 (July–December 1965):111–22; rpt. *Revista de la Universidad de México* 34, no. 1 (September 1979):9–14.

43. Poniatowska, "El terrón," p. 140.

44. Cervera, "Entrevista," pp. 10–11.

45. See Avilés, "Juan Rulfo," pp. 1, 4.

46. Dimas Lidio, "Rulfo: 'He dejado de publicar, pero nunca dejaré de escribir,'" *El Gallo Ilustrado,* no. 419 (5 July 1970). See also Bruce-Novoa, "Some Answers," p. 476.

Chapter Two

1. For a study and examples of the story of the Mexican Revolution see my anthology, *Cuentos de la Revolución* (México: UNAM, 1976).

2. For an analysis of "El llano en llamas" see Chapter 3.

3. Carlos Landeros, "Charla con Juan Rulfo," *Diorama de la Cultura,* Sunday Supplement of *Excélsior* (Mexico City), 6 March 1966, p. 1. It is interesting to compare this observation by Rulfo with what Revueltas had said in 1962:

I had not read [Faulkner] before I wrote *El luto humano* and it was only after I had published this book, and precisely because critics had spoken about a rather considerable, and suspicious, influence of Faulkner over that novel, that I read *As I Lay Dying,* and [the novel] gave me an enormous surprise, and at the same time it was an extraordinary stimulus for me. To be sure, keeping in mind the distances regarding Faulkner's artistic level . . . I found that there existed certain common characteristics between Faulkner and me regarding a certain tormented sensibility about strikingly similar preoccupations. However, what was considered a direct influence from Faulkner over my work is nothing but a question of thematic and ambiental correspondences. (*El Gallo Ilustrado,* Sunday Supplement of *El Dia,* Mexico City, 9 September 1962).

4. Howard Mancing, in his article "The Art of Literary Allusion in Juan Rulfo," *Modern Fiction Studies* 23 (1977):242–44, states that he found only one literary allusion in Rulfo's works, an allusion that he traces back to *Lazarillo de Tormes.* It is the phrase "Así, de día se tapaba el agujero y de noche se volvía a abrir," which appears in the story "¡Diles que no me maten!"

5. Emmanuel Carballo, "Arreola y Rulfo," *Revista de la Universidad de México* 8, no. 7 (March 1954):28.

6. "La vida no es muy seria en sus cosas," *América, Revista Mensual, Tribuna de la Democracia* 40 (30 June 1945):35–36. Photocopy in my files. According to Harss (pp. 256–57) this story was first published in the Guadalajara review *Pan* in 1942. This cannot possibly be since *Pan* did not appear until 1945 (see José Luis Martínez, *Literatura mexicana siglo XX, 1910–1949. Segunda Parte: Guías Bibliográficas* [México: Antigua Librería Robredo, 1950], p. 167).

7. As stated by Rulfo himself (see Chapter 1) this story is all that remains of his first unpublished novel. This statement is repeated in a note in *El Cuento: Revista de Imaginación* 8, no. 47 (July 1971):134, where the story is reproduced (pp. 137–43).

8. "Un pedazo de noche. Fragmento," in Juan Rulfo, *Antología personal*. Prólogo de Jorge Ruffinelli (México, 1978), p. 146. This story first appeared in the *Revista de Literatura Mexicana*, Nueva Epoca, no. 3 (September 1959), pp. 7–14; also in Juan Rulfo, *Pedro Páramo y El llano en llamas* (Barcelona, 1969), pp. 267–75. It has not been translated.

9. "La vida no es muy seria en sus cosas," in *Antología personal*, p. 156. This story has not been translated.

10. Donald K. Gordon, *Los cuentos de Juan Rulfo* (Madrid, 1976), p. 24.

Chapter Three

1. *Pan: Revista de Literatura* was edited in Guadalajara by Juan José Arreola and Antonio Alatorre. Only seven numbers appeared, between June 1945 and January–February 1946 (see Martínez, *Literatura,* p. 167). *América* was founded in Mexico City in 1942 by Roberto Guzmán Araujo and Marco Antonio Millán. The subtitle, *Revista Mensual, Tribuna de la Democracia,* was changed with number 56 (1948) to *Revista Antológica* (see Marco Antonio Millán, *"América: Revista Antológica," Las Revistas Literarias de México. Segunda Serie* [México: Instituto Nacional de Bellas Artes, 1963], pp. 113–35).

2. The story "Es que somos muy pobres" must have been published in another periodical since it does not appear in *Pan: Revista de Literatura,* Guadalajara, Jalisco, as do "Nos han dado la tierra," no. 2 (July 1945), n.p., and "Macario," no. 6 (November 1945), n.p. I owe this information to José Luis Martínez of Mexico City and take this opportunity to thank him for his prompt reply to my inquiry regarding the rare periodical *Pan.*

3. Roffé, *Juan Rulfo,* p. 56.

4. *El llano en llamas* (México, 1953), tr. George D. Schade as *The Burning Plain* (Austin, 1967). All further quotations from this work are from this translation.

5. "La cuesta de las comadres," *América* 55 (February 1948):31–38; "Talpa," *América* 62 (January 1950):79–81; "El llano en llamas," *América* 64

(December 1950):68–85; "¡Diles que no me maten!" *América* 66 (August 1951):125–30.

6. *The Burning Plain,* pp. 3–8.

7. William Faulkner, *The Sound and the Fury* (New York: Random House, 1946), p. 23. See James E. Irby, *La influencia de William Faulkner en cuatro narradores hispanoamericanos* (México, 1956), pp. 137–40.

8. Aspects of this story have been studied by M. A. Serna Maytorena, "Elementos plásticos y cromáticos en 'Macario' de Juan Rulfo," *Boletín del Instituto de Literatura* (La Plata), boletín 2 (March 1972):43–55; Inés Gónima, "'Macario' de Juan Rulfo, una visión insólita del mundo a través del lenguaje," *Razón y Fábula* (Bogotá, Colombia), no. 29 (May–August 1972), pp. 38–58; Stephanie M. Robbins, "Yuxtaposición como técnica en un cuento de Juan Rulfo: 'Macario,'" *Insula* 25 (September 1970):10; Luis Fernández Veas Mercado, "Macario," *Nueva Narrativa Hispanoamericana* 4 (1974):275–82; also, "Fundamentos lingüísticos y psicológicos del monólogo interior en 'Macario' de Juan Rulfo: el monólogo interior como una visión del mundo," *Revista Canadiense de Estudios Hispánicos* 1 (1977):272–81; J. P. Shapiro, "Une Histoire Contée par un idiot . . . W. Faulkner et J. Rulfo," *Revue de Littérature Comparée* 53 (1979):338–47.

9. "They Gave Us the Land," in *The Burning Plain,* pp. 11–16.

10. See Nathan L. Whetten, *Rural Mexico* (Chicago: University of Chicago Press, 1948), p. 89.

11. See Howard F. Cline, *Mexico, Revolution to Evolution, 1940–1960* (New York: Oxford University Press, 1963), Chapter 22.

12. Aspects of this story have been studied by Gordon, *Cuentos,* pp. 59–62; M. A. Serna Maytorena, "Integración de hombre y paisaje en 'Nos han dado la tierra,'" *Et Caetera,* 2a época, 6, no. 21 [55] (July–September 1971):13–22; Arno Ros, *Zur Theorie literarischen Erzählens. Mit einer Interpretation der "cuentos" von Juan Rulfo* (Frankfurt, 1972), pp. 170–73; Buenaventura Piñero Díaz, "Juan Rulfo: 'Nos han dado la tierra' y el 'problema' de las vanguardias," *Letras,* Instituto Universitario Pedagógico de Caracas 32–33 (1976):159–77.

13. "The Hill of the *Comadres,*" in *The Burning Plain,* pp. 19–28. This story has been analyzed by Ros, *Zur Theorie,* pp. 167–70; Gordon, *Cuentos,* pp. 63–70; Floyd Merrel, "Towards a New Model of Narrative Structure (Applied to Rulfo's 'La cuesta de las comadres')," in Mary Ann Beck et al., eds., *The Analysis of Hispanic Texts: Current Trends in Methodology* (Jamaica, N.Y., 1976), pp. 150–69.

14. *Antología personal,* p. 145.

15. Harss and Dohmann, "Juan Rulfo," p. 266.

16. "We're Very Poor," in *The Burning Plain,* pp. 31–37.

17. The method was used earlier by Manuel Gamio in his book *The Mexican Immigrant, His Life-Story. Autobiographic Documents Collected by . . .* (Chicago: University of Chicago Press, 1931).

18. See Enrique Pupo-Walker, "La transposición de valores pictóricos en la narrativa de Ferretis y Rulfo," *Nueva Narrativa Hispanoamericana* 1 (1971):95–103.

19. "Talpa," in *The Burning Plain*, pp. 65–75. This story has been analyzed by Ros, *Zur Theorie*, pp. 149–57, *Cuentos*, pp. 32–39; Graciela B. Coulson, "Observaciones sobre la visión del mundo en los cuentos de Juan Rulfo: a propósito de 'Talpa' y 'No oyes ladrar los perros,'" *Nueva Narrativa Hispanoamericana* 1 (1971):159–66; Stephen T. Clinton, "Form and Meaning in Juan Rulfo's 'Talpa,'" *Romance Notes* 16 (1975):520–25; Lilia Pérez González, "'Talpa,' relato de Juan Rulfo: una reflexión sobre la muerte," *Explicación de textos literarios* 5 (1976):23–28.

20. Although the name Zenzontla is fictitious it could very easily pass for the name of a town in Jalisco, for it is made up of the Nahuatl words *centzontli* ("mockingbird") and *tlan* ("place"). In the novel *Pedro Páramo* the geographical name of Contla is also fictitious.

21. For a study of point of view in "Talpa" see Gordon, *Cuentos*, pp. 32–39.

22. Enrique Vázquez, "Una entrevista con Juan Rulfo," *La Gaceta* 7, no. 82 (October 1977):18–19 (taken from *Somos*, Buenos Aires, 24 December 1976). "Talpa" has also been adopted for the ballet under the name "La Manda" [The offering].

23. "The Burning Plain," in *The Burning Plain*, pp. 79–95. It first appeared in *América* 64 (1950):68–85.

24. Roffé, *Juan Rulfo*, p. 63.

25. "Juan Rulfo examina su narrativa," *Escritura: teoría y crítica literaria* 2 (1976):305.

26. See Vicente T. Mendoza, *El romance español y el corrido mexicano* (México: Imprenta Universitaria, 1939), pp. 508–10. The second one, according to Mendoza, was composed in the year 1913; the first either in 1916 or later, according to the date given in the first verse. Both are reproduced in Mendoza's *Lírica narrativa de México* (México: UNAM, 1964), pp. 110–12.

27. Petronilo Flores, from Sinaloa, joined the Revolution in 1913 and sided with Obregón against Villa. He was commander of the 17th Regiment; died in 1957, as Governor of the Territory of Baja California Sur. In the story, the narrator attributes to Petronilo Flores the derailment, robbing, and burning of a train at the Hill of Sayula, an historical incident also mentioned by Juan José Arreola in his novel *La feria* (México: Joaquín Mortiz, 1963), p. 22.

28. General Agustín Olachea, a native of Lower California, fought under Obregón; later Governor of Territory of Baja California Sur, and twice of Baja California Norte.

29. For a study of point of view in "El llano en llamas" see Gordon, *Cuentos*, pp. 70–91.

30. For a comparison of Rulfo and the writers of the Revolution see Max Aub, *Guía de narradores de la Revolución Mexicana* (México: Fondo de Cultura

Económica, 1969), pp. 58–62, and Manuel Durán, "Los cuentos de Juan Rulfo o la realidad trascendida," in Enrique Pupo-Walker, ed., *El cuento hispano-americano ante la crítica* (Madrid, 1973), pp. 195–214.

31. Aspects of "El llano en llamas" have been studied by E. P. Mocega-González, "La Revolución y el hombre en el cuento 'El llano en llamas,'" *Cuadernos Americanos* 38, no. 4 (July–August 1979):215–29; Gutiérrez Marrone, *Estilo,* pp. 92–112; Gabriele von Munk Bento, "El ambiente rural en 'El llano en llamas' de Juan Rulfo, en su limitación y trascendencia," *Literatura iberoamericana: influjos locales.* Memoria del X Congreso del Instituto Internacional de Literatura Iberoamericana (México: UNAM, 1965), pp. 123–29; Ros, *Zur Theorie,* pp. 145–49. Hugo Rodríguez Alcalá, *El arte de Juan Rulfo* (México, 1965), pp. 61–89.

32. "Tell Them Not to Kill Me!" in *The Burning Plain,* pp. 99–107. An earlier translation of this story is that of Lysander Kemp, in *New World Writing, 14,* a Mentor Book (New York: The New American Library, 1958), pp. 116–22.

33. Cervera, "Entrevista," p. 10. "¡Diles que no me maten!" first appeared in *América* 66 (August 1951):125–30.

34. "Juan Rulfo," recorded readings by the author of two of his own stories, "¡Diles que no me maten!" and "Luvina." Presentación by Carlos Blanco Aguinaga. México: UNAM, 1963.

35. The Colonel never appears in the story; however, his voice is heard by all as he speaks from inside the barracks. This device tends to assuage the guilt of the Colonel for his cruel order to kill the old man after thirty-five years of penance.

36. Aspects of this story have been studied by Gordon, *Cuentos,* pp. 145–54, and Gary Brower, "'¡Diles que no me maten!': aproximación a su estructura y significado," *Nueva Narrativa Hispanoamericana* 3, no. 2 (September 1973):231–35.

Chapter Four

1. Mocega-González, "La Revolución," p. 214.
2. Roffé, *Juan Rulfo,* p. 56.
3. "The Man," in *The Burning Plain,* pp. 41–51.
4. For an analysis and other examples of this type of story see my article "El héroe acosado," *Revista de la Universidad de México* 33, no. 8 (April 1979):25–28.
5. See my articles "El realismo mágico en la literatura hispanoamericana," *Cuadernos Americanos* 26, no. 4 (1967):230–35, and "El realismo mágico y la nueva narrativa hispanoamericana," in Donald W. Bleznick, ed., *Variaciones interpretativas en torno a la nueva narrativa hispanoamericana* (Santiago, Chile: Helmy F. Giacoman, Editor, 1972), pp. 49–62. See also Lorraine Elena

Ben-Ur, "El realismo mágico en la crítica hispanoamericana," *Journal of Spanish Studies—Twentieth Century* 4, no. 3 (Winter 1976):150–63; Lucila-Inés Mena, "Hacia una formulación teórica del realismo mágico," *Bulletin Hispanique* 77 nos. 3–4 (1975):395–407; Dieter Janik, "Der 'realismo mágico': zur Bedeutung des Magischen im hispanoamericanischen Gegenwartsroman," in Johannes Hösle and Wolfgang Eitel, eds., *Beiträge zur vergleichenden Literaturgeschichte: Festschrift für Kurt Wais zum 65 Geburtstag* (Tübingen: Niemeyer, 1972), pp. 375–87; Donald A. Yates, ed., *Otros mundos, otros fuegos: fantasía y realismo mágico en Iberoamérica* (Lansing: Michigan State University Press, 1975).

6. Aspects of "El hombre" have been studied by ·Gordon, *Cuentos,* pp. 161–67; Marcelo Coddou, "Fundamentos para la valoración de la obra de Juan Rulfo (Preposiciones para la interpretación y análisis del cuento 'El hombre')," *Nueva Narrativa Hispanoamericana* 1 (1971):139–58.

7. "At Daybreak," in *The Burning Plain,* pp. 55–61. Aspects of this story have been studied by Rodríguez Alcalá, *Arte,* pp. 11–27; "Estudio estilístico de 'En la madrugada' de Juan Rulfo," *Hispanic Review* 34 (1966):228–41; "Un cuento entre dos luces: 'En la madrugada' de Juan Rulfo," *Actas del Segundo Congreso de Hispanistas* (Nimega, 1967), pp. 499–512; Ros, *Zur Theorie,* pp. 157–64; Gordon, *Cuentos,* pp. 168–77.

8. "Luvina," in *The Burning Plain,* pp. 111–21. An earlier translation of this story is that of Joan and Boyd Carter, in *Prairie Schooner* 31 (1957–1958):300–306; rpt. *Mexican Life* 34, no. 3 (March 1958):11–12, 64.

9. For an extended analysis of this story see my article "El cuento de ambiente: 'Luvina' de Juan Rulfo," *Nivel* 38 (25 February 1962):4; rpt. *Homenaje a Juan Rulfo,* ed. Helmy F. Giacoman (New York, 1974), pp. 91–98; also Ros, *Zur Theorie,* pp. 164–75; Gordon, *Cuentos,* pp. 91–102; Rodríguez Alcalá, *Arte,* pp. 43–60; Carlota B. Cannon, "'Luvina' o el ideal que pudo ser: en torno a un cuento de Juan Rulfo," *Papeles de Son Armadans* 80 (1976):203–16; Nahum Meggel, "Fondo indígena y problemática moderna en 'Luvina' de Juan Rulfo," *Nueva Revista Filológica Hispánica* 27 (1978):103–12.

10. "The Night They Left Him Alone," in *The Burning Plain,* pp. 125–29.

11. In the Schade translation the reading is: "The ground clouded his thoughts" (p. 125). And also, "Now, climbing, he saw the ground again" (p. 125). However, the Spanish edition reads: "El sueño le nublaba el pensamiento," and "Ahora, en la subida, lo vio venir de nuevo." See Juan Rulfo, *El llano en llamas,* Cuarta Edición, Colección Popular (México, 1959), p. 105. The translation of *sueño* as "ground" could be due to the fact that, four lines above, the word *suelo* ("ground") appears in Spanish: "Allí iban los tres, con la mirada en el suelo" (p. 105). Henceforth, quotations in Spanish will be from this edition.

12. See Gordon, *Cuentos,* pp. 154–59.

13. "Remember," in *The Burning Plain,* pp. 133–36.

14. See Gordon, *Cuentos,* pp. 39–42; Ros, *Zur Theorie,* pp. 181–83; Mary L.

Thomas, "A Stylistic Study of 'Acuérdate' by Juan Rulfo," *South Atlantic Bulletin* 42, no. 4 (1977):57–66.

15. "No Dogs Bark," *The Burning Plain*, pp. 139–43.

16. Unfortunately, this distinction is lost in translation.

17. For an extended analysis of this story see Rodríguez Alcalá, *El arte*, pp. 20–42; his "Bajo el peso de la cruz," *Recopilación*, pp. 72–83; and "En torno a un cuento de Juan Rulfo: 'No oyes ladrar los perros,'" in Giacoman, *Homenaje*, pp. 121–33; Roland Forgues, "La técnica del suspenso dramático en un cuento de Juan Rulfo: 'No oyes ladrar los perros,'" *Letras de Deuste* 6 (1976):175–85; Gordon, *Cuentos*, pp. 124–28. In 1975 a motion picture based on this story was presented at the Cannes Festival, as an entry from Mexico.

18. "Paso del Norte," in *The Burning Plain*, pp. 147–56.

19. "Juan Rulfo examina su narrativa," p. 309.

20. "Anacleto Morones," in *The Burning Plain*, pp. 159–75.

21. See Fausto Castillo, "Cuando el teatro no es teatro," *México en la Cultura* 575 (20 March 1960), p. 8.

22. Beatriz Reyes Nevares, *The Mexican Cinema* (Albuquerque: University of New Mexico Press, 1976), p. 165.

23. This story has been analyzed by Gordon, *Cuentos*, pp. 102–13; Ros, *Zur Theorie*, pp. 184–85; Barry W. Munn, "Juan Rulfo's 'Anacleto Morones,'" *Reflexión* 2 (1973):51–56.

24. "The Day of the Landslide," tr. Hardie St. Martin, *Doors and Mirrors: Fiction and Poetry from Spanish America, 1920–1970*, eds. Hortence Carpentier and Janet Brof (New York, 1972), pp. 223–24. All quotations from this story are from this translation.

25. Juan Rulfo, *El llano en llamas*, Segunda edición (México, 1970), pp. 136–44. First published in *México en la Cultura* 334 (14 August 1955):3, 5; rpt. *Anuario del cuento mexicano 1955* (México: INBA, 1956), pp. 291–99.

26. See Gordon, *Cuentos*, pp. 136–44; Ros, *Zur Theorie*, pp. 195–96; Patricio Ríos-Segovia, "'El día del derrumbe' y su textura humorística," *American Hispanist* 2, no. 13 (1976):11–13.

27. "[The Inheritance of] "Matilde Arcángel,"" tr. Margaret Shedd, *Kenyon Review* 28 (1966):187–93. All quotations from this story are from this translation. This work has been published under two different titles, "La herencia de Matilde Arcángel" and "La presencia de Matilde Arcángel." Under the first title it first appeared in *Cuadernos Médicos* 1, no. 5 (March 1955):57–61, and was reprinted in *Anuario del cuento mexicano 1959* (México: INBA, 1960), pp. 218–22; and with the second in *Metáfora* 1, no. 4 (Mexico City, September–October 1955):27–32.

28. In some Spanish versions this character is called Tranquilino Herrera, and Euremio is called Ereutemio. In the Shedd translation Euremio is called Emeterio.

29. See Gordon, *Cuentos*, pp. 136–44.

Chapter Five

1. Carlos Fuentes, *La nueva novela hispanoamericana* (México: Joaquín Mortiz, 1969), p. 16.
2. For a study of the development of the Mexican novel see John S. Brushwood, *Mexico in Its Novel* (Austin: University of Texas Press, 1966).
3. Avilés, "Juan Rulfo opina," p. 1.
4. Ernest Moore, *Bibliografía de novelistas de la Revolución mexicana* (México: n.p., 1941), p. 8.
5. Ibid., p. 10.
6. Octavio Paz, "Letras de México: una nueva novela mexicana," *Sur* 12, no. 105 (July 1943):93.
7. Claude Couffon, *Hispanoamérica en su nueva literatura,* tr. from the French by José Corrales Egea (Santander: Publicaciones de la Isla de los Ratones, 1962), p. 75.
8. Octavio Paz, "Landscape and the Novel in Mexico," in his *Alternating Current,* tr. Helen R. Lane (New York: Viking Press, 1973), pp. 15–16.
9. Rafael Solana, "El dato humano," *El Popular,* 12 June 1938, p. 5, as quoted by Adalbert Dessau, *La novela de la revolución mexicana* (México: Fondo de Cultura Económica, 1972), p. 123. The Botas Stable refers to the editorial house of Andrés Botas, who published most if not all of the novels of the Revolution.
10. Manuel Pedro González, *Trayectoria de la novela en México* (México: Editorial Botas, 1951), p. 92.
11. Manuel Pedro González, "La novela hispanoamericana en el contexto de la internacional," in *Coloquio sobre la novela hispanoamericana* (México: Fondo de Cultura Económica, 1967), pp. 63–64.
12. Couffon, *Hispanoamérica,* pp. 85–86.
13. María Embeita, "Octavio Paz: poesía y metafísica," *Ínsula,* nos. 260–61 (July–August 1968), p. 12.
14. Octavio Paz and Julián Ríos, *Solo a dos voces* (Barcelona: Editorial Lumen, 1973), p. [7].
15. Marta Portal, *Proceso narrativo de la Revolución mexicana* (Madrid: Ediciones Cultura Hispánica, 1976).
16. See Chapter 2.
17. Juan Rulfo, "La tierra pródiga," *Revista Mexicana de Cultura,* Sunday Supplement of *El Nacional,* Segunda Época, no. 919 (8 November 1964), p. 6.
18. See note 42 of Chapter 1.
19. Avilés, "Juan Rulfo opina," p. 1.
20. Ibid.
21. For an extended discussion of the place of *Pedro Páramo* in contemporary Mexican fiction see Luis Mario Schneider's study "*Pedro Páramo* en la novela mexicana: ubicación y bosquejo," in Ángel Flores y Raúl Silva Castro, eds., *La novela hispanoamericana actual* (New York, 1971), pp. 123–44.

22. Roffé, *Juan Rulfo,* pp. 38, 41.
23. Ibid., p. 60.
24. Ramírez, "Style and Technique," p. 15.
25. Roffé, *Juan Rulfo,* pp. 60–61.
26. Personal conversation with Juan Rulfo, Guadalajara, 24 June 1962.
27. See Juan Rulfo, "Un cuento," in *Las Letras Patrias* 1 (January–March 1954):104. This change in the name of the town was first commented upon by Ricardo Estrada in his article "Los indicios de *Pedro Páramo," Universidad de San Carlos* (Guatemala), no. 65 (1965); rpt. *Recopilación de textos sobre Juan Rulfo,* pp. 110–32. Quotations are from this reprint. Both Estrada and Gordon (pp. 113–21) analyze "Un cuento" as if it were an independent short story. Although there are important variants between this prose and the first chapter of *Pedro Páramo,* they cannot be considered as two different works, since the variants are not structural or thematic.
28. Roffé, *Juan Rulfo,* p. 61. Although there is no town by that name in Jalisco, there is a Comala in the neighboring state of Colima. It is situated at the foot of the Volcán del Fuego.
29. Ibid., p. 32.
30. Estrada, "Los indicios," p. 117.
31. Roffé, *Juan Rulfo,* p. 61.
32. Rodríguez Alcalá, *El Arte,* p. 48.
33. Roffé, *Juan Rulfo,* p. 32. For the relationship between the stories and the novel see Estrada's article; Irby's chapter on Rulfo; Lanin A. Gyurko, "Rulfo's Aesthetic Nihilism: Narrative Antecedents of *Pedro Páramo," Hispanic Review* 40 (1972):451–66; Ferrer Chivite, "*El llano en llamas,* antecedentes de *Pedro Páramo,*" part 2 of his *El laberinto mexicano en/de Juan Rulfo;* George Ronald Freeman, *Paradise and Fall in Rulfo's "Pedro Páramo": Archetypal and Structural Unity* (Cuernavaca, 1970).
34. Barbara L. C. Brodman, *The Mexican Cult of Death in Myth and Literature* (Gainesville: University Presses of Florida, 1976), p. 48.
35. Roffé, *Juan Rulfo,* p. 31.
36. Harss and Dohmann, "Juan Rulfo," p. 250.
37. René Girard, *Violence and the Sacred,* tr. Patrick Gregory (Baltimore: John Hopkins University Press, 1977), p. 255.
38. Roffé, *Juan Rulfo,* p. 31.

Chapter Six

1. Personal conversation with Juan Rulfo, Guadalajara, 24 June 1962.
2. Juan Rulfo, *Pedro Páramo,* tr. Lysander Kemp (New York, 1959), p. 50. Further quotations are from this translation, Evergreen Book E-149.
3. Juan Rulfo, "Los murmullos" [fragment of the unpublished novel *Los Murmullos*], *Revista de la Universidad de México* 8, no. 10 (June 1954):6–7.
4. Joseph Sommers, "Los muertos no tienen tiempo ni espacio (un diálogo

con Juan Rulfo)," in *La narrativa de Juan Rulfo,* ed. Joseph Sommers (México, 1974), p. 19.

5. See Alfred J. MacAdam, "Juan Rulfo, the Secular Myth," in his *Modern Latin American Narrative* (Chicago: University of Chicago Press, 1977), pp. 88–90, where he discusses the role of Pedro Páramo as a mythical king.

6. Roffé, *Juan Rulfo,* p. 65.

7. Ibid., pp. 65–66.

8. Ibid., pp. 66, 69.

9. Alí Chumacero, "El *Pedro Páramo* de Juan Rulfo," *Recopilación,* p. 109. This review was first published in the *Revista de la Universidad de México* 9, no. 8 (April 1955):25, 26, 27.

10. Irby, "Juan Rulfo," p. 161.

11. John S. Brushwood and José Rojas Garcidueñas, *Breve historia de la novela mexicana* (México: Ediciones De Andrea, 1959), p. 140.

12. Brushwood, *Mexico in Its Novel,* p. 32.

13. Carlos Blanco Aguinaga, "Realidad y estilo de Juan Rulfo," in Sommers, *Narrativa,* p. 107. This article was first published in the *Revista Mexicana de Literatura* 1, no. 1 (1955):59–86.

14. Mariana Frenk, *"Pedro Páramo,"* in Sommers, *Narrativa,* pp. 31–43; Luis Leal, "La estructura de *Pedro Páramo,"* in Sommers, *Narrativa,* pp. 44–54; Rodríguez Alcalá, *Arte,* pp. 113–26; Didier T. Jaén, "La estructura lírica de *Pedro Páramo,"* *Revista Hispánica Moderna* 33 (1967):224–31; C. Enrique Pupo-Walker, "Rasgos del lenguaje y estructuras en *Pedro Páramo,"* *Papeles de Son Armadans* 57, no. 170 (May 1970):117–36.

15. Since Blanco Aguinaga published his article in 1955, critics have been speaking of the structure of the novel as divided into two parts, the first part ending with the death of Juan Preciado; however, such a simple division ignores the rich and complex interrelations that exist between the narrative sequences.

16. Sommers, *Narrativa,* p. 19.

17. Cf. Freeman, *Paradise and Fall.*

18. For a discussion of bird imagery as symbolic of the fallen condition of man see Floyd Merrell, "Some Considerations of Bird Imagery in Rulfo's *Pedro Páramo,"* *Romance Notes* 17 (1977):255–59. For a study of the function of animals in Rulfo's short stories see Luis A. Jiménez, "Funcionalidad de los animales en *El llano en llamas,"* in Gladys Zaldívar, ed., *Cinco aproximaciones a la narrativa hispanoamericana* (Madrid: Playor, 1977), pp. 109–32.

Chapter Seven

1. See Chapter 1.

2. See Beatriz Reyes Nevares, *The Mexican Cinema. Interviews with Thirteen Directors.* Tr. Elizabeth Gard and Carl J. Mora. Introduction by E. Bradford Burns (Albuquerque: University of New Mexico Press, 1976).

3. Jorge Ayala Blanco, "Presentación y notas," in Juan Rulfo, *El gallo de oro y otros textos para cine* (México, 1980), p. 14. All quotations are from this first edition.

4. José de la Colina, "El cine: recuento de 1965," *Revista de la Universidad de México* 20, no. 4 (December 1965):26.

5. *Tiempo* 46, no. 1183 (4 January 1965):31.

6. Personal conversation with Juan Rulfo, Guadalajara, 15 June 1962.

7. Translated from the Spanish by Anita Brenner under the title *Sunburst* (New York: Viking Press, 1944).

8. Ambrose Bierce, "An Occurrence at Owl Creek Bridge," in *In the Midst of Life and Other Stories,* a Signet Classic (New York: New American Library, 1961). The story, in Spanish under the title "El ahorcado," was published in Mexico in the periodical *El Cuento* 1, no. 6 (October 1964). Rulfo is a member of the editorial board.

9. Jorge Luis Borges, "El milagro secreto," in *Ficciones* (Buenos Aires: Emecé, 1956), pp. 159–67.

10. *El gallo de oro*, p. 119.

11. See Selected Bibliography, Secondary Sources, part 2.

12. "Situación actual de la novela contemporánea" (1965). See Selected Bibliography, Primary Sources, part 2.

13. "Juan Rulfo examina su narrativa," *Escritura* 2 (1976):305–17.

14. See *Excélsior,* Mexico City, 27 September 1980.

15. See Selected Bibliography, Primary Sources, part 2.

16. "Situación actual de la novela," p. 115.

17. Ibid.

18. Ibid., p. 115–16.

19. Ibid., p. 116.

20. Ibid.

21. Ibid., p. 118.

22. Ibid., p. 119.

23. Ibid., p. 120.

24. Ibid., p. 122.

25. "Juan Rulfo examina su narrativa," p. 309.

26. Ibid., p. 313.

Selected Bibliography

This bibliography contains: (1) works by Rulfo; (2) book-length studies; (3) selected studies from which quotations have been taken or which are mentioned in the notes; (4) articles not found in the existing bibliographies, mentioned below.

PRIMARY SOURCES

1. Novels

El gallo de oro y otros textos para cine. Presentación y notas de Jorge Ayala Blanco. México: Ediciones Era, 1980. Contents: "El gallo de oro," "El despojo," "La fórmula secreta."

Pedro Páramo. México: Fondo de Cultura Económica, 1955; paperback edition (Colección Popular), 1964. Numerous reprints; edición escolar, edited by Luis Leal. New York: Appleton, 1970. Special edition revised by author. México: Fondo de Cultura Económica, 1980.

Pedro Páramo y El llano en llamas. Barcelona: Editorial Planeta, 1969. Includes also "Un pedazo de noche," "El día del derrumbe," and "La herencia de Matilde Arcángel."

Pedro Páramo; El llano en llamas. Prólogo de Felipe Garrido. México: Clásicos de la Literatura, 1979.

2. Fragments of Novels

"Un cuento." *Las Letras Patrias* 1 (January–March 1954): 104–8; rpt. *Anuario del cuento mexicano 1954.* México: Instituto Nacional de Bellas Artes, 1955 [fragment of novel *Pedro Páramo*].

"Los murmullos." *Revista Universidad de México* 8, no. 10 (June 1954):6–7 [fragment of novel *Pedro Páramo*].

"Un pedazo de noche (Fragmento)." *Revista Mexicana de Literatura.* Nueva Época 3 (September 1959):7–14. Dated January 1940; rpts. *Humboldt* 13 (1972):25–27; *El Cuento* 8 (July–August 1971):137–43.

3. Short Stories

"La cuesta de las comadres." *América* 55 (February 1948):31–38.

116

"El día del derrumbe." *México en la Cultura,* no. 334 (14 August 1955), 3, 5; rpts. *Anuario del cuento mexicano 1955.* México: INBA, 1956, pp. 291–99; *Crónicas de Latinoamérica.* Buenos Aires: Editorial Jorge Álvares, 1968, pp. 13–24.

"¡Diles que no me maten!" *América* 66 (August 1951):125–30.

"La herencia de Matilde Arcángel." *Cuadernos Médicos* 1, no. 5 (March 1955):57–61; rpt. *Anuario del cuento mexicano 1959.* México: INBA, 1960, pp. 218–22.

"El llano en llamas." *América* 64 (December 1950):66–85.

El llano en llamas. México: Fondo de Cultura Económica, 1953; paperback edition (Colección Popular), 1959; 2a. edición corregida y aumentada, 1970. Contains two new stories, "El día del derrumbe" and "La herencia de Matilde Arcángel"; "El Paso del Norte," from first edition, not included. Numerous reprints. Also with *Pedro Páramo.* See Novels.

"Macario." *Pan,* no. 6 (November 1945), n. pag.; *América* 48 (June 1946):67–72.

"Nos han dado la tierra." *Pan* (Guadalajara), no. 2 (July 1945), n. pag.

"Talpa." *América* 62 (January 1950):79–81.

"La vida no es muy seria en sus cosas." *América* 40 (1945):35–36; rpt. *El Cuento* 12 (April–September 1978):712–14; *Antología personal,* pp. 153–56.

4. Anthologies

Antología personal. Prólogo de Jorge Ruffinelli. México: Editorial Nueva Imagen, 1978. Contents: eight short stories from *El llano en llamas;* two selections from *Pedro Páramo,* "Un pedazo de noche," and "La vida no es muy seria en sus cosas."

5. Other Prose Writings

Prólogo y Selección. *Noticias históricas de la vida y hechos de Nuño de Guzmán.* Vol. 1, *Libros y documentos para la historia de la Nueva Galicia.* Guadalajara, Jalisco: Círculo Occidental, 1962.

Review. *Tres cuentos* by Agustín Yáñez. *Bulletin* (Centro Mexicano de Escritores) 11, no. 4 (May 1964):4.

Review. *La ruta de la libertad* by Fernando Benítez. *Bulletin* (Centro Mexicano de Escritores) 11, no. 4 (May 1964):4.

Review. *La tierra pródiga* by Agustín Yáñez. *Revista Mexicana de Cultura.* Sunday Literary Supplement of *El Nacional,* México, 2a. Época, no. 919 (8 November 1964), p. 6.

Review. *Los palacios desiertos* by Luisa Josefina Hernández. *Books Abroad* 38 (Summer 1964):294.

"Situación actual de la novela contemporánea." *ICACH* (Instituto de Ciencias y Artes de Chiapas, Tuxtla Gutiérrez) 15 (July–December 1965):111–22. Rpt. *Revista de la Universidad de México* 34, no. 1 (September 1979):9–14.

Discurso al recibir el Premio Nacional de Letras 1970. *El Día* (México), 26
    November 1970, p. 10.
"Juan Rulfo examina su narrativa," [Lecture transcribed by María Helena
    Ascanio]. *Escritura* 2 (1976):305–17.
"Dos textos" [María Lombardo de Caso; Elizabeth Strebel]. *Texto Crítico* 6 nos.
    16–17 (January–June 1980):37–39.

6. Translations (English only; for other languages see Ramírez).
"Anacleto Morones." See "The Miraculous Child."
"Because We Are Very Poor." Translated by Lysander Kemp. In: Ángel Flores,
    ed. *Great Spanish Short Stories.* New York: Dell Publishing Co., 1962;
"Because We're So Poor." Translated by Henry Dyches. *Mexico Quarterly
    Review* (México) 1, no. 3 (Summer 1962):166–69.
The Burning Plain and Other Stories. Translated by George D. Schade. Austin:
    University of Texas Press, 1967. Pan American Paperback Edition. 3rd
    Printing, 1978.
"The Day of the Landslide." Translated by Hardie St. Martin. In: Hortence
    Carpentier and Janet Brof, eds. *Doors and Mirrors. Fiction and Poetry from
    Spanish America, 1920–1970.* New York: Grossman Publishers, 1972, pp.
    223–29.
"La herencia de Matilde Arcángel." Translated by Margaret Shedd. *Kenyon
    Review* 28, no. 2 (1966):187–93.
"The Hill of the *Comadres.*" Translated by Lysander Kemp. *Atlantic* 213 (March
    1964):102–5.
"Luvina." Translated by Joan and Boyd Carter. *Prairie Schooner* 31, no. 4
    (Winter 1957–1958):300–306, and in *Mexican Life* 34, no. 3 (March
    1958):11–12, 64.
"Macario." Translated by George D. Schade. *Texas Quarterly* 2, no. 1 (Spring
    1959):48–51; also in Thomas Cranfill, ed. *The Muse in Mexico.* Austin:
    University of Texas Press, 1959, pp. 48–51.
"The Miraculous Child" ["Anacleto Morones"]. Translated by Irene Nicholson.
    Encounter 5, no. 3 (September 1955):13–19; translated by Anna West.
    Chelsea Review 6 (Winter 1960):47–59 (under title "Anacleto Morones").
"The Night They Left Him Behind." Translated by Robert Cleland. *Mexican
    Life* 32, no. 11 (November 1956):17–18.
"No Dogs Bark." Translated by George D. Schade. *Texas Quarterly* 2, no. 1
    (Spring 1959):52–55; also in *The Muse in Mexico,* pp. 52–55.
Pedro Páramo. Translated by Lysander Kemp. New York: Grove Press, 1959.
"Talpa." Translated by Robert Cleland. *Mexican Life* 33, no. 1 (January
    1957):62, 64; translated by Darwin J. Flakoll and Claribel Alegría, eds.
    New Voices of Spanish America. Boston: Beacon Press, 1962, pp. 32–39;
    translated by J. A. Chapman. In: Jean Franco, ed. *Short Stories in Spanish/
    Cuentos Hispánicos.* Harmondsworth, Middlesex, England: Penguin

Books, 1966, pp. 167–87 [bilingual ed.]; translated by Pat M. Ness, ed. *Contemporary Latin American Short Stories*. Greenwich, Conn.: Fawcett Publications, 1974.

"Tell Them Not to Kill Me!" Translated by Lysander Kemp. In: *New World Writing, 14*, A Mentor Book. New York: American Library Association 1958.

"They Gave Us the Land." Translated by Jean Franco. *Encounter* 25, no. 3 (September 1965):15–17; also in J. M. Cohen, ed. *Latin American Writing Today*. Baltimore: Penguin Books, 1967.

SECONDARY SOURCES

1. Bibliographies

Foster, David William. "Rulfo, Juan." *Mexican Literature: A Bibliography of Secondary Sources*. Metuchen, N.J., & London: The Scarecrow Press, 1981, pp. 306–23.

Gutiérrez Marrone, Nila. "Bibliografía." In her *El estilo de Juan Rulfo; estudio lingüístico*. New York: Bilingual Press, 1978, pp. 125–76. Follows Ramírez's bibliography, with some additions.

Lioret, E. Kent. "Continuación de una Bibliografía de y sobre Juan Rulfo." *Revista Iberoamericana* 40, no. 89 (October–December 1974):693–705. Supplements Ramírez's bibliography.

Ramírez, Arthur. "Hacia una bibliografía de y sobre Juan Rulfo." *Revista Iberoamericana* 50, no. 86 (January–March 1974):135–71. First and most comprehensive bibliography of Juan Rulfo.

2. Criticism (for studies of individual short stories see notes of Chapters 3 and 4)

Álvarez, Nicolás Emilio. "Structuralism and *Pedro Páramo*: A case in Point." *Kentucky Romance Quarterly* 24 (1977):419–31. After pointing out the limitations of structuralism, and advocating the study of the novel in its social and historical context, goes on to analyze it utilizing the concept of binary oppositions.

Anich, Dorothea. "Tratamiento del tiempo en *Pedro Páramo*." *Et Caetera*, 2a. Época 6, no. 21 [55] (1971):23–31. A consideration of chronological and narrative time in the novel.

Arango L., Manuel A. "Correlación social entre el caciquismo y el aspecto religioso en la novela *Pedro Páramo*." *Cuadernos Hispanoamericanos* 341 (1978):401–12. Using internal evidence, the author traces the relations between Pedro Páramo, the cacique, and Father Rentería, the representative of the other political power, the Church.

Armand, Octavio. "Sobre las comparaciones en Rulfo." *Nueva Narrativa Hispanoamericana* 2 (1972):172–77. Rpt. in Giacoman, *Homenaje* . . . , pp. 335–46. Discusses the presence and function of nature in Rulfo's fiction, as observed in the use of similes and comparisons, especially with stones.

Bastos, María Luisa, and Molloy, Sylvia. "La estrella junto a la luna: variantes de la figura materna en *Pedro Páramo.*" *Modern Language Notes* 92 (1977):246–68. A study of the function of women in the novel, especially in their relation to Juan Preciado: the mother-son relationship, as seen from a mythological perspective.

———. "El personaje de Susana San Juan: clave de la enunciación y de enunciados en *Pedro Páramo.*" *Hispamérica* 7, no. 20 (1978):3–24. Complements the previous study. Cf. José de la Colina, below.

Bell, Alan S. "Rulfo's *Pedro Páramo:* A Vision of Hope." *Modern Language Notes* 81 (1966):238–45. Perhaps the only critic who finds a note of optimism in the novel. Pedro Páramo is unable to conquer Susana San Juan.

Blanco Aguinaga, Carlos. "Realidad y estilo de Juan Rulfo." *Revista Mexicana de Literatura* 1 (1955):59–86. Rpt. Sommers, *La narrativa* . . . , pp. 88–116; *Nueva novela latinoamericana,* pp. 85–113. Edited by Jorge Lafforgue. Buenos Aires: Editorial Paidos, 1969. First important overview of Rulfo's fiction; helped to orient succeeding criticism.

Burton, Julianne. "Sexuality and the Mythic Dimension in Juan Rulfo's *Pedro Páramo.*" *Symposium* 28 (1974):228–47. Detailed analysis of the sexual dimension of the novel.

Camacho, Mario Ovidio. "La muerte en la narrativa de Rulfo." In: *Actas de la Quinta Asamblea Interuniversitaria de Filología y Literaturas Hispánicas,* Universidad Nacional del Sur, Argentina, 1968, pp. 69–73. The thematic importance of death in Rulfo's fiction.

Carballo, Emmanuel. "Arreola y Rulfo." *Revista de la Universidad de México* 8, no. 7 (March 1954):28–29, 32; rpt. in *Recopilación* . . . , pp. 133–44; and in part in Sommers, *La narrativa* . . . , pp. 23–30. Comparative study of authors as short-story writers.

Chumacero, Alí. "El *Pedro Páramo* de Juan Rulfo." *Revista de la Universidad de México* 9, no. 8 (April 1955):25, 26–27; rpt. *Recopilación* . . . , pp. 106–9. First important review by well-known poet. Criticizes the novel's lack of coherence. Had influence over critics such as Irvy, Rojas Garcidueñas, José Agustín, Gustavo Sainz, etc.

Colina, José de la. "Susana San Juan (El mito femenino en *Pedro Páramo*)." *Revista de la Universidad de México* 19, no. 8 (April 1965):19–21; rpt. Sommers, *La narrativa* . . . , pp. 60–66. Archetypal study of feminine characters in novel. Cf. Bastos and Molloy article, above.

Cortés Gaviño, Agustín, and Landa Guevara, Antonio. "Notas sobre *El luto humano* y *Pedro Páramo.*" *Revista de Bellas Artes,* Nueva Época 9 (May–June

1973):65–72. A comparison of Revueltas's and Rulfo's novels, giving emphasis to thematic similarities (death, solitude, etc.).

Crow, John A. *"Pedro Páramo:* A Twentieth Century Dance of Death." In: *Homenaje a Irving A. Leonard.* Edited by Raquel Chang-Rodríguez and Donald A. Yates. East Lansing: Latin American Center, Michigan State University, 1977, pp. 219–27. Brief enumeration of principal characteristics of novel.

Didier, Jaén T. "La estructura lírica de *Pedro Páramo." Revista Hispánica Moderna* 33 (1967):224–31. Stresses the spatial structure of the novel.

Dorfman, Ariel. "En torno a *Pedro Páramo* de Juan Rulfo." *Mapocho* 5 (1966):289–95; rpt. in his *Imaginación y violencia en América.* Santiago, Chile: Editorial Universitaria, 1970, pp. 181–92; also in Giacoman, *Homenaje . . . ,* pp. 147–58. A critical review of Rodríguez Alcalá, *El arte de Juan Rulfo.*

Durán, Manuel. "Juan Rulfo cuentista: la verdad casi sospechosa." *Nueva Narrativa Hispanoamericana* 1, no. 2 (September 1971):167–74; rpt. Giacoman, *Homenaje . . . ,* pp. 109–20. A discussion of Rulfo's works in the context of the writers of the Revolution, and a comparison of the story "Anacleto Morones" and the novel *Pedro Páramo.*

———. "Los cuentos de Juan Rulfo o la realidad trascendida." In *El cuento hispanoamericano ante la crítica.* Edited by Enrique Pupo-Walker. Madrid: Editorial Castalia, 1973, pp. 195–214. An elaboration of the above study.

Embeita, María J. "Tema y estructura en *Pedro Páramo." Cuadernos Americanos* 25:151, no. 2 (March–April 1967):218–23. Points out the skillful use that Rulfo has made of realistic and phantasmagoric motifs.

Estrada, Ricardo. "Los indicios de *Pedro Páramo." Universidad de San Carlos* (Guatemala) 65 (1965), 67–85; rpt. *Recopilación . . . ,* pp. 110–32. A lengthy discussion of the principal elements (structure, themes, motifs, literary devices) that give the novel its aesthetic quality.

Fernández, Sergio. "El mundo paralítico de Juan Rulfo." *Filosofía y Letras* (México) 27, nos. 53–54 (January–June 1954):259–69; rpt. in his *Cinco escritores hispanoamericanos.* Mexico: UNAM, 1958, pp. 113–41. A perceptive study flawed by the insistence on considering the characters as Indians motivated by a pseudo-Indian psychology.

Ferrer Chivite, Manuel. *El laberinto mexicano en/de Juan Rulfo.* México: Organización Editorial Novaro, 1972. A study of Rulfo's fiction as a mirror of his life, based on Octavio Paz's ideas about solitude. Both works are studied as a unit.

Franco, Jean. "El viaje al país de los muertos." In: Sommers, *La narrativa . . . ,* pp. 117–40. The world of the novel is seen as representing a social and moral order in the process of changing to a new system. The conflicts are the result of the mixture of the old and the new.

Freeman, George Ronald. *Paradise and Fall in Rulfo's "Pedro Páramo":* Ar-

chetype and Structural Unity. Cuernavaca, México: Centro Intercultural de Documentación, 1970 (CIDOC: Cuaderno, 47). A study of the novel as a fictional archetype of the myth of the fall from Paradise. Some attention given to the short stories.

Frenk, Mariana. "Pedro Páramo." *Revista de la Universidad de México* 15, no. 11 (July 1961):18, 19, 20, 21; rpt. *Recopilación* . . . , pp. 84–95; Sommers, *La narrativa* . . . , pp. 31–43. A study of the novel's characters, spatial structure, and language. One of the earliest attempts to understand its complex nature.

Fuentes, Carlos. "Pedro Páramo." *L'Esprit des Lettres* (Oullins, Rhône) 6 (November–December 1955):74–76; translated and reprinted by Joseph Sommers in his *La narrativa* . . . , pp. 57–59. A brief review pointing out how the novel differs from those of the Revolution, the function of nature, and the popular characteristic of its style.

Gallo, Marta. "Realismo mágico en *Pedro Páramo.*" In: *Otros mundos y otros fuegos: fantasía y realismo mágico en Iberoamérica.* Edited by Donald A. Yates. East Lansing: Michigan State University, Latin American Studies Center, 1975, pp. 103–11. The integration of history and the magical is what gives form to the novel.

Giacoman, Helmy F., ed. *Homenaje a Juan Rulfo.* New York: Las Américas, 1974. A collection of twenty-three essays, some of which are listed separately in this bibliography.

Gordon, Donald K. *Los cuentos de Juan Rulfo.* Madrid: Playor, 1976. An overview of all of Rulfo's stories classified according to their narrative point of view.

Gyurko, Lanin A. "Rulfo's Aesthetic Nihilism: Narrative Antecedents of *Pedro Páramo.*" *Hispanic Review* 4 (1972):451–66. An analysis of the similarities between the characters of the short stories and the novel, giving emphasis to the function of fatalism.

Harss, Luis, and Dohmann, Barbara. "Juan Rulfo, or the Souls of the Departed." In their *Into the Mainstream.* New York: Harper and Row, 1967, pp. 246–75. First important interview revealing aspects of Rulfo's life in relation to his works.

Hill, Deane E. "Integración, desintegración e intensificación en los cuentos de Juan Rulfo." *Revista Iberoamericana* 34, no. 66 (1968):331–38; rpt. Giacoman, *Homenaje* . . . , pp. 99–108. Discovers that Rulfo's stories are organized around images that denote integration, disintegration, or intensification.

Irby, James E. "Juan Rulfo." In his *La influencia de William Faulkner en cuatro narradores hispanoamericanos.* México: n.p., 1956, pp. 132–63. First to point out Faulkner's influence on Rulfo.

Juan Rulfo: homenaje nacional. México: Instituto Nacional de Bellas Artes/SEP, 1980. Collection of articles with 100 photographs by Rulfo. Deluxe edition.

Leal, Luis. "Juan Rulfo." In: *Narrativa y crítica de nuestra América,* pp. 258–86. Edited by Joaquín Roy. Madrid: Editorial Castalia, 1978. An overview of Rulfo's life and works.

Luraschi, Ilse A. "Narradores en la obra de Juan Rulfo: estudio de sus funciones y efectos." *Cuadernos Hispanoamericanos* 308 (February 1976):5–29. A detailed analysis of point of view and its function in the creation of a new vision of reality.

Lyon, Ted. "Ontological Motifs in the Short Stories of Juan Rulfo." *Journal of Spanish Studies, Twentieth Century* 1 (1973):161–68. The ontological motifs used in *El llano en llamas* are seen in relation to the world created by Rulfo.

MacAdam, Alfred J. "Juan Rulfo: the Secular Myth." In his *Modern Latin American Narrative.* Chicago: University of Chicago Press, 1977, pp. 88–90. Brief mythical interpretation of *Pedro Páramo.*

Mancing, Howard. "The Art of Literary Allusion in Juan Rulfo." *Modern Fiction Studies* 23 (1977):242–44. Traces the only literary allusion used by Rulfo, in the story "¡Diles que no me maten!", back to the picaresque novel *Lazarillo de Tormes.*

Mena, Lucila Inés. "Estructura narrativa y significado de *Pedro Páramo.*" *Cuadernos Americanos,* no. 217 (1978), pp. 165–88. A discussion of the novel's structure and its relation to the world of Comala (history, paradise, purgatory).

Merrell, Floyd. "Towards a New Model of Narrative Structure Applied to Rulfo's 'La cuesta de las comadres.'" In: *The Analysis of Hispanic Texts: Current Trends in Methodology.* Edited by Mary Ann Beck et al. Jamaica, N.Y.: Bilingual Press, 1976, pp. 150–69. Uses Rulfo's story to illustrate a critical model for fiction, based on the idea of "deep meaning."

Miró, Emilio. "Juan Rulfo." *Cuadernos Hispanoamericanos,* no. 246 (June 1970), pp. 600–37; rpt. Giacoman, *Homenaje . . . ,* pp. 207–45. A thematic survey of Rulfo's narrative in the context of Spanish American fiction. Each story is discussed.

Ortega, Julio. "*Pedro Páramo.*" *Comunidad Latinoamericana de Escritores* (México, D.F.), boletín no. 2 (October 1969), pp. 3–9; rpt. in his *La contemplación y la fiesta: notas sobre la novela latinoamericana actual,* pp. 17–30; also in Giacoman, *Homenaje . . . ,* pp. 135–45, and Sommers, *La narrativa . . . ,* pp. 76–87. A mythic interpretation of the novel.

Peralta, Violeta, and Befumo Boschi, Liliana. *Rulfo: la soledad creadora.* Buenos Aires: Fernando García Cambeiro, 1975. Analysis of Rulfo's fiction utilizing semiological concepts.

Pupo-Walker, Enrique. "Tonalidad, estructuras y rasgos del lenguaje en *Pedro Páramo.*" In: Giacoman, *Homenaje . . . ,* pp. 159–71. Points out that antithesis is the prevailing rhetorical device used in the novel.

Recopilación de textos sobre Juan Rulfo. Habana: Casa de las Américas, 1969. Serie Valoración Múltiple. A collection of fifteen essays, some of which are listed separately in this bibliography.

Rodríguez Alcalá, Hugo. *El arte de Juan Rulfo.* México: INBA, 1965. First extensive study of Rulfo's fiction. The novel and four stories are analyzed. The thematic approach predominates.

Roffé, Reina, ed. *Juan Rulfo. Autobiografía armada.* Buenos Aires: Ediciones Corregidor, 1973. Initially published in the periodical *Latinoamérica* 1 (December 1972). An integrated collection of answers to questions submitted to Rulfo during various interviews and arranged in the form of an autobiography.

Ros, Arno. *Zur Theorie literarischen Erzählens. Mit einer Interpretation der "cuentos" von Juan Rulfo.* Frankfurt: Athenäum Verlag, 1972. Makes use of Rulfo's stories to expound a narrative theory.

Sánchez, Porfirio. "Relación entre la negación del tiempo y el espacio y Comala en *Pedro Páramo.*" *Cuadernos Americanos* 203 (1975):212–21. Points out that Rulfo, by presenting the characters as dead, is able to abolish time and space.

Schneider, Luis Mario. "*Pedro Páramo* en la novela mexicana: ubicación y bosquejo." In: *La novela hispanoamericana actual.* Edited by Ángel Flores and Raúl Silva Castro. New York: Las Américas, 1971, pp. 123–44. Rulfo's works viewed in the context of Mexican fiction.

Serna Maytorena, M. A. "Integración de hombre y paisaje en 'Nos han dado la tierra.'" *Et Caetera* (Guadalajara), 2a. Época 6, no. 21 [55] (July–September 1971):13–22. A study of the relations between characters and their Jalisco environment.

Serra, Edelweiss. "Estructura de *Pedro Páramo.*" *Nueva Narrativa Hispanoamericana* 3, no. 2 (September 1973):211–29. A discussion of the metonymical organization of the narrative units (*microrelatos*) of the novel.

Sommers, Joseph. "Through the Window of the Grave: Juan Rulfo." *New Mexico Quarterly* 38 (1968):84–101; rpt. in his *After the Storm. Landmarks of the Modern Mexican Novel.* Albuquerque: University of New Mexico Press, 1968, pp. 69–94; also in Giacoman, *Homenaje . . .* , pp. 39–59 (taken from the Spanish translation of *After the Storm* which appeared under the title *Yáñez, Rulfo, Fuentes: la novela mexicana moderna.* Caracas: Monte Ávila Editores, 1969, pp. 93–123). Demonstrates how technique, style, and mythic substructure combine to project an implicit world outlook.

———, ed. *La narrative de Juan Rulfo.* México: Sep-Setentas, 1974. A collection of twelve essays, most of which are listed separately in this bibliography.

Vasconcelos, Diva. "*Pedro Páramo:* notas de uma leitura." *Vozes* 65, no. 7 (September 1971):537–42. Apropos the Portuguese translation of *Pedro Páramo.* The novel is considered an example of fantastic literature, as defined by Todorov.

Zapata Olivella, Manuel. "La atmósfera psicoantropológica en la novelística de Juan Rulfo." *Boletín Cultural y Bibliográfico del Banco de la República* (Bogotá, Biblioteca Luis Ángel Arango) 11 (1968):143–46. Advances the theory that in order to penetrate Rulfo's fiction it is necessary to study the regional culture of which he is a product.

Index